# THE ECONOMIC IMPACT OF LEASING

# The Economic Impact of Leasing

David G. Mayes
*Head of Statistics and Head of Computing*
*National Economic Development Office, London*

and

Clive S. Nicholas
*Continuing Education and Training Officer*
*University of Exeter*

MACMILLAN
PRESS

First published 1988

Published by
THE MACMILLAN PRESS LTD
Houndmills, Basingstoke, Hampshire RG21 2XS
and London
Companies and representatives
throughout the world

Printed in Hong Kong

British Library Cataloguing in Publication Data
Mayes, David G.
The economic impact of leasing.
1. Leases—Great Britain   2. Great –
Britain—Economic conditions—1945–
I. Title   II. Nicholas, Clive S.
330.941′0858      HC256.6
ISBN 0–333–44195–8

# Contents

*Preface*                                           vii

1  Introduction                                        1

2  The Growth of Leasing in the UK                    13

3  Leasing from the Viewpoint of the Lessor           27

4  The Use of Leasing by Firms                        57

5  Leasing and the Incentive to Invest               87

6  Econometric Evidence                              107

7  The Experience in Other Countries                 127

8  The Future of Leasing in the UK                   145

9  Conclusions                                        155

*Notes*                                               162

*References*                                          165

*Index*                                               169

# Preface

This book was born when David Mayes was Editor at the National Institute of Economic and Social Research in London, in 1980. Part of the Editor's task is to run the team of economists and the econometric model which the Institute uses in its forecasting. At that time we found considerable difficulty in forecasting investment by manufacturing industry, although, of course, we were aware of leasing and its extremely rapid rate of growth.

In the version of the National Institute model then in use – Interim Model IV – leasing was incorporated as a specific item which was added to manufacturing investment and subtracted from investment by the distribution and services sectors. The argument was that leased assets were treated by the user (lessee) in the same way as owned assets. Hence, the appropriate behavioural relationship was to add together investment and leased assets for manufacturing, on the one hand, and to subtract leased assets from the investment undertaken by the owners (lessors) in the distribution and service sectors.[1]

However, this arrangement did not work well. Our equations tended to underforecast manufacturing investment. Despite the rapid fall in profits in manufacturing in the early 1980s and the very high levels of interest rates, both nominal and real, investment including leasing ran at a higher level than we expected. The reason was thought to be clear. Because lessors could offset the whole of their investment against tax it was possible for them to offer relatively attractive terms to lessees, hence, in effect, cutting the cost of investment. Under these circumstances investment could be expected to increase relative to what it would otherwise have been.

Even this was not enough in 1980–1. David Mayes, working with Gay Wenban-Smith (who was responsible for the investment sector at the Institute), suggested that, as taxable profits in manufacturing fell, the number of companies which could benefit from leasing would increase. Similarly, for each company, leasing would become attractive at an earlier point (see Mayes and Wenban-Smith, 1981).

Having the hypothesis was one thing, being able to prove it was quite another. Investment behaviour could have changed for any one or more of a number of reasons, of which the rise of leasing was only one. The National Institute did not have the resources to study the problem so we looked elsewhere for a grant.

The Equipment Leasing Association quickly saw the benefit of the research and offered us financial support to undertake a survey of its members, but we still had to look further for the main funding. Several bodies, including the SSRC, were not convinced of the need for the work but we persevered and eventually in 1984 we were lucky enough to get a substantial grant from the Leverhulme Trust. It is perfectly true to say that without this our research would not have been possible. We hope the Trust approves of what we have been able to achieve with the money, although it should be made clear that it is in no way responsible for the work itself or the views expressed.

By that time neither Gay nor David were working for the National Institute. Gay was with British Gas and not in a position to participate, and David was Head of Statistics at the National Economic Development Office. Fortunately, as an Honorary Research Fellow at the University of Exeter, it was possible for David to undertake the work in the Department of Economics there. It was even more fortuitous to be able to recruit Clive Nicholas as the Research Fellow to work full-time on the project, since he had not only graduated from Exeter but had also been working in the finance industry in the South West with experience of leasing. The chance of finding such an economist who was available at that precise time and place must have been infinitesimal.

We should like to record our thanks here to the large number of people in the leasing industry, in particular, and in the firms in manufacturing industry who took the trouble to fill in our questionnaires. Response rates exceeded our best hopes, perhaps indicating that some felt our work to be worth while. Everyone gave of their time freely, we hope they think we have used it valuably.

It is probably invidious to single out individuals for their contribution, but we must mention the Equipment Leasing Association, especially its Secretary-General, Basil Damer, his two assistants, Charles Ferrier and Andrew Thompson, and its Chairman during the main part of the work, David Beever. The Equipment Leasing Association gave us the opportunity to reach a wider audience. However, tribute for enabling us to inflict our ideas on others must also go to Robert Hawkins of the *Leasing Digest*, who arranged for us to talk at the Lease-Europe meeting in Frankfurt, in 1981, as well as at the World Leasing Congress in London, in 1985.

One disadvantage of the long delay caused by the struggle to obtain finance was that no sooner had the project got under way than the 1984 Finance Bill was introduced, proposing the reduction of 100 per cent capital allowances to a standard 25 per cent writing down allowance. The irony of working on a project to establish the contribution of leasing to the economy, both through increasing the rate of economic growth and through helping to ease the effects of recessions by its countercyclical behaviour, while the government removed the most important single incentive for leasing, was not lost on us. No doubt it was lost on the Chancellor of the Exchequer. I suppose we must thank him for raising the general level of awareness about leasing and its importance. It was, however, rather disconcerting to realise the number of people, overseas as well as in the UK, who regarded leasing as partly a tax fiddle, or not quite as respectable as other, more traditional ways of raising finance for investment.

Now that the research has been completed and the transition envisaged in the 1984 Finance Act has finished, it is more difficult to judge the appropriate use to which the findings can be put. It is clear that leasing has led to a higher rate of investment, which even though it may not have been as productive as the Chancellor would have liked, nevertheless contributed to raising the UK's rate of economic growth. Cyclical stabilisation also appears to be somewhat out of fashion. Here the findings of the research, although positive, were somewhat weaker. The availability of leasing clearly affects the timing of investment as was illustrated by massive surges in the level of leasing in the first quarters of 1985 and 1986 as people tried to beat the two downward steps in initial tax allowances.

It is unrealistic to expect the current government to unwind its legislation, but may lead it to treat leasing more favourably in the future, say, by permitting leveraged leases. No doubt other financial innovations will arise to help fill the gap. The work may also be a pointer to future governments looking for a way to stimulate manufacturing industry.

It would be normal at this point to thank the typist, but it was Clive who attacked the word processor and produced the final report. It is a tribute to this new technology that it has been possible to transport the discs round the world to New Zealand, where David Mayes was Director of the NZ Institute of Economic Research, insert them in a computer and edit the text for this book.

We had various alarums and excursions in performing the computer analysis, which was not aided by geographical separation. We record our thanks to Philip Frater and Sarah Clokie at NEDO, Keith

Cuthbertson at the University of Newcastle upon Tyne, Hassan Feisal at NIESR, Paul Fisher at the ESRC Econometric Modelling Bureau at the University of Warwick, whose facilities were-used for simulating the National Institute model, and Phil Briggs at NZIER. We are grateful to David Walker and others at Exeter for advice as the project progressed. We are unable to blame any of the aforementioned for the result, which remains our own responsibility. We enjoyed doing the work, we hope others enjoy reading about it.

DAVID G. MAYES
CLIVE S. NICHOLAS

# 1 Introduction

The major reform of the corporation tax system implemented in the 1984 Finance Act has radically altered the economics of equipment leasing in the UK. Fundamental changes in capital allowances and corporation tax have not only given rise to considerable discussion about the future of leasing as a source of asset finance, but have also focused attention on its past role in the economy.

Since the early 1970s there has been a remarkably rapid expansion in the use of leasing by firms to finance capital expenditure. Accompanying this growth has been the development of an extensive and specialised leasing industry which has become an increasingly significant source of capital formation. Assets leased to manufacturers by companies in the financial sector increased sixfold in real terms over the decade 1972 to 1982 (from £160 million to £1014 million in constant 1980 prices), and rose from 2.5 per cent to 18.5 per cent as a proportion of total manufacturing investment.[1]

## 1.1 THE ROLE OF TAX INCENTIVES

The rapid growth of leasing has been significantly influenced by the system of tax investment incentives based on capital allowances. These are intended to encourage investment by increasing the after-tax rate of return to the firm. They permit firms to offset their capital expenditure against their taxable profits thereby reducing their corporation tax liability. This cuts costs and improves cash flow in the period immediately after making the investment, thus aiding the firm in the difficult period between incurring the cost of investment and receiving the profits it is designed to generate. Clearly if there are insufficient taxable profits to utilise available capital allowances immediately, particularly in periods of high inflation, the tax benefit will be lower and will fall further in value the longer it has to be postponed.

During the 1970s an increasing number of firms, especially in the manufacturing sector, accumulated tax allowances greater than profits. Several factors were responsible for this. On the one hand, the introduction of the 100 per cent allowance for plant and machinery which offset the entire cost of the investment against tax in the first year together with other concessions, such as that for stock relief, increased the allowances available as inflation rose. On the other hand, a general downturn in profitability decreased the sum against which they could be offset. In these conditions firms had no corporation tax liability and, because they could carry forward un-used allowances to offset against future profits, were likely to remain in this position of 'tax exhaustion' for a considerable period.

However, not all firms in the economy experienced tax exhaustion. Others, especially those in the financial sector which had not been adversely affected by inflation and high interest rates in the same way, had maintained profitability and therefore had the profits, or 'taxable capacity', against which capital allowances could be offset.

Leasing provided a solution to this imbalance. Firms with taxable capacity, principally in the financial sector, were able to purchase assets and lease them out to firms in other sectors. By so doing both were able to benefit from the tax advantages of capital allowances in some proportion. The effect of claiming capital allowances on such assets was to defer tax liability for the financial firm. This tax benefit was passed on in part to the user in the form of lease payments which were lower than the equivalent payments for borrowing the money for investment. The lessor retained the remainder of the benefit for its own profit. Therefore, by leasing, tax-exhausted firms were able to capture much of the benefit of capital allowances in the form of asset finance which was effectively lower in cost than other types of finance.

The phasing out of first-year capital allowances and the move to a standard 25 per cent writing down allowance on investment in plant and machinery, resulting from the 1984 Finance Act, has serious implications for leasing. The removal of these allowances will make leasing more expensive and will generally increase the cost of capital to firms. Against this there is a simultaneous reduction in the rate of corporation tax which will reduce the tax liability of those firms which are not tax exhausted. The picture is therefore complex. Some firms with high profits, which would not have been tax exhausted in any case, will now have lower tax bills because of the lower allowances, and firms which would have been tax exhausted will not now be able to obtain the use of further assets through leasing at such cheap rates as before, nor will financial firms with taxable capacity be able to reduce their own tax liabilities or offer such favourable leasing rates as previously. It is largely against this background that the present study has been undertaken.

## 1.2 THE MOTIVATION FOR THE STUDY

Although the substantial increase in the use of leasing since the early 1970s has led to a growing academic and professional interest in this form of finance, until now much of the existing study of the subject has been primarily concerned with leasing as a financial decision-making problem from the perspective of the individual user firm or analysis of the working and structure of the leasing industry.[2] Little attention has as yet been given specifically to the wider examination of the impact of the growth of leasing on the economy as a whole and, in particular, to its possible effects on investment.[3] Undoubtedly part of the increased use of leasing by firms has arisen from displacement of other sources of finance but there is prima facie evidence to indicate that leasing may actually have directly influenced levels of capital expenditure in the economy. During the late 1970s and early 1980s actual investment including leased assets, especially in the manufacturing sector, maintained a higher level than forecast by some econometric models. This suggests that leasing might play a role in investment behaviour above that of simply providing an alternative source of finance to firms. It may result in more invest-ment and hence in a faster rate of economic growth and higher income per head. The purpose of our study has therefore been to determine the nature of this relationship, namely, the effects of leasing on the investment behaviour of firms and its macroeconomic implications.

## 1.3 THE NATURE OF LEASING

Today leasing is used to describe transactions ranging from the short-term hire of a motor vehicle to the renting of major items of oil extraction and processing plant and equipment. Despite the wide diversity of leasing activity, the basic concept is in fact very simple. In return for specified payments (rentals) the owner of an asset (the lessor) grants exclusive use of it for an agreed period to the hirer (the lessee). Leasing is thus a method of financing the use of an asset without actually purchasing it. The fundamental characteristic of a leasing agreement is the division of the use and ownership of an asset into distinct legal and economic activities. Under existing UK legisla-tion the lessor remains legal owner whilst the lessee has right to economic use providing that the terms of the agreement are maintained.[4] Unlike the practice in some other countries an option for the lessee to purchase the leased asset may not be given.[5] This distinction is very important for it is this which makes leasing a unique form of financial instrument and from which the economic effects of leasing are largely generated. If ownership could be transferred then leasing would be largely indistinguishable from hire purchase and the benefits of capital allowances would not accrue to the lessor.

It is now common in the leasing industry to structure leasing agreements to suit the particular requirements of the lessor and lessee with the result that many forms of agreement exist. However, it is generally accepted that leases may be broadly divided into two broad categories – finance leases and operating leases. Finance leasing and operating leasing differ widely both in practice and in underlying economic rationale.

### 1.3.1 Finance Leasing

In finance leasing the role of the lessor is principally limited to the provision of finance to enable the firm to obtain the use of an asset. It is therefore carried out mainly by financial institutions, such as banks and their leasing subsidiaries, although in recent years large companies outside the financial sector have engaged in finance leasing when they had taxable capacity. The initial investment decision to acquire an asset and the choice of supplier are made by the lessee. The asset is purchased by the lessor. Rentals in the leasing agreements are calculated to allow the lessor to recover the cost of the asset and to make a profit. Payments are spread over a primary period which does not extend beyond the useful life of the asset and hence the residual value at the end of this period is not of significance to the lessor. However, it is important to the lessor that the lease is not terminated before the primary period is completed as many assets do not have a ready resale market nor clearly determinable resale value. Finance leases therefore tend to include quite heavy penalties for early cancellation to try to avoid encountering these difficulties or costs. At the end of the primary period the asset may be sold to a third party, in which case the lessee receives a major proportion of the sale proceeds as a 'rebate of rentals', or a secondary period of leasing may be agreed with nominal rentals. Throughout the lease, insurance and maintenance are the responsibility of the lessee. A finance lease in effect 'transfers substantially all the risks and rewards of ownership of an asset to the lessee'[6] and, although legal ownership remains with the lessor, is similar to purchase using other forms of instalment debt.

### 1.3.2 Operating Leasing

Operating leasing is very different. It is concerned with the provision of a complete service to the lessee rather than simply a financial arrangement. Operating lessors are typically specialists in the types of asset they lease out and possess a detailed knowledge of equipment and equipment markets. The asset is purchased, maintained and insured by the lessor who will often hold stocks of such assets. Unlike finance leasing, the lessor does not recover the asset cost over a single lease period. Profit may derive from leasing the asset over a number of relatively short periods to successive lessees, from ancilliary arrangements (such as service contracts), or from the sale of the asset. The residual value of the asset is consequently of considerable importance and, because of the alternatives of re-leasing or selling available to the lessor, an operating lease is not normally difficult to cancel. While a finance lease effectively transfers the risks and rewards of ownership to the lessee, with an operating lease these risks, especially obsolescence, are borne by the lessor. Operating leasing is therefore widely used in relation to assets such as computers where technological development is rapid.

Although a clear distinction has been drawn between operating leasing and finance leasing, in practice many leasing contracts contain elements of both forms and are not easily categorised. Nevertheless, the distinction is of significance for, as the descriptions of finance leasing and operating leasing imply, different types of leasing may be used for varying reasons and not all forms of leasing will have precisely the same effects on investment.


## 1.4 WHY FIRMS LEASE

At the microeconomic level, the effects of leasing on investment behaviour will be largely influenced by the underlying reasons why firms decide to use this method of finance. Leasing presents a range of advantages to the firm and it might be expected that the reasons firms use leasing will tend to vary widely depending on the particular conditions experienced by the individual firm when the decision to lease is made.

The advantages generally attributed to leasing include:

## 1. An Additional Source of Finance

It finances the use of an asset without using existing resources. A leasing agreement can cover the full cost of an asset and payment is spread over a period so avoiding lump sum expenditure. Existing resources are conserved which may be utilised for other purposes and cash flow advantages arise.

## 2. Lower Cost

If a firm has insufficient taxable profits to be able to absorb capital allowances immediately, leasing provides a mechanism for recovering part of the benefit in the form of reduced rental payments. This can effectively lower the cost of finance to the firm and enables it to gain from investment tax incentives which otherwise might be eroded in value or ultimately forgone.

## 3. Reductions in Risk

Certain risks may be reduced through the use of leasing. An operating lease, for example, transfers the risks of ownership such as technological obsolescence away from the firm to the lessor. Leasing can also form a hedge against inflationary increases in the cost of capital assets by enabling the firm to acquire the use of an asset with rentals based on current costs and to fund such rental payments from future and possibly inflated earnings.

## 4. Longer-term Finance

Large sums of finance for sizeable investment programmes, such as those encountered in the oil industry, can be raised over relatively long terms through leasing which may not be forthcoming from other sources. Financial institutions may prefer to fund by leasing secured on specific assets rather than by other forms of lending.

## 5. Improved Portfolio Balance

Leasing is an alternative source of finance to the firm and can assist in forming a balance of funding between various forms of funding operations. It is also commonly held that leasing can increase the debt capacity of the firm.

## 6. *Ease and Flexibility*

Compared with other sources of finance, leasing is often easier to arrange and the form of agreement can be very flexible. Payment of rentals may be structured to meet revenue patterns which can be beneficial to cash flow.

## 7. *Off-balance Sheet*

Although changes have been announced in the publication of 'Statement of Standard Accounting Practice No. 21' (SSAP 21), in August 1984, concerning the disclosure of finance leases in the accounts of the lessee, leasing has been considered an off-balance sheet form of finance which does not affect balance sheet gearing ratios.

## 8. *Avoids Controls*

It can provide finance which may not be available from other sources as a result of institutional factors. In periods of strict credit control, leasing may be exempt from regulation or there may simply exist a shortage of medium-term finance from financial institutions.

## 9. *Fixed Agreement*

Leasing is a fixed form of agreement which can ease administration, budgetary accuracy and cash flow forecasting.

## 10. *Revenue Not Capital Account Transaction*

Leasing rentals are met from revenue and so it is possible to avoid capital expenditure limits or borrowing restrictions.

Each of these advantages may to varying degrees have an effect on the investment behaviour of firms. The decision to invest is likely to be influenced by a range of internal and external factors relating not only to past and present conditions but also to expectations of the future. Furthermore, the firm does not normally operate in what would be described as a 'free market' but faces financial, organisational and technological constraints which will affect the investment process and the volume of investment undertaken. These include the structure of existing assets and liabilities, operating limits laid down by principal creditors, capital expenditure limits, indivisability of large capital items and the need for compatibility with existing plant and machinery. Leasing presents a further option to the decision-maker when considering investment opportunities, and as such may enable investment to occur that might not otherwise have taken place or may enable the timing of the investment decision to be brought forward.

Advantages such as the avoidance of lump sum expenditure, convenience and flexibility can facilitate the investment process. Although some of these factors appear to be minor and may perhaps arguably apply rather more to the small rather than large firm, their cumulative effects on investment may be significant.

Whilst it is true that the influence of financial variables upon investment has been the subject of considerable debate and conflicting evidence,[7] it remains arguable that both the availability and the cost of finance may have an effect on investment.

Leasing is an additional source of finance which may assist in the optimal use of available funds by the firm. More efficient use of finance could imply increased investment. Leasing will also influence investment behaviour if funds are not available from other sources. A general shortage of medium-term finance or indeed reluctance on the part of financial institutions to fund large projects through other forms of finance are widely reported examples of such market imperfections.

However, there is a further aspect of leasing in relation to the availability of finance which arises from its effects upon the debt capacity of the firm. In theory, leasing and debt are held to be equivalent and consequently leasing will displace debt on a 'pound for pound' basis. Given the existence of an optimal capital structure of debt to equity for the firm and limits on the willingness of lenders to provide finance above certain levels of risk, it should be the case that leasing cannot increase the debt capacity of the firm. Nevertheless, this does not appear to be the case in practice. Previous surveys of lessee behaviour have found a large number of instances where leasing is an additional source which can increase the level of finance available to the firm.[8]

Several reasons have been put forward to explain this apparent inconsistency.[9] Potential lenders may have imperfect knowledge of the leasing commitments of firms and therefore be willing to extend credit. Prior to the introduction of SSAP 21 there was no obligation on the part of lessees to disclose leasing agreements in their published accounts, and leasing had long been considered an 'off-balance sheet' form of finance. However, given the growth of leasing in the UK and accounting recommendations before SSAP 21, it seems unlikely that lenders would ignore leasing completely.

Nevertheless, the anomaly has persisted. An alternative explanation might be found in the suggestion that leasing involves less risk than other forms of finance, as the asset may be more easily recovered if the lessee defaults and therefore lessors might be willing to 'lend' more than would be the case with other types of finance. A further possibility is that leasing would be expected to increase debt capacity if no optimal debt–equity structure exists. Each of these explanations is open to question and yet in practice leasing does appear to be utilised to expand debt capacity. In situations where borrowing limits have been reached firms tend to regard leasing as a further source of finance.

Leasing has also influenced the cost of finance to the firm. As mentioned earlier, tax considerations have played a major part in the growth of leasing. In addition to the capture of unused capital allowances already described, it is possible for a firm to bring forward the benefits of capital allowances by using a lessor with an earlier year end than its own. If leasing results in the reduction of the cost of finance then it may increase the level of investment.

## 1.5 MACROECONOMIC EFFECTS

At the macroeconomic level, leasing may have had a significant effect on the level and timing of investment. As we have seen, leasing was in part a response to distortions in the system of taxation and investment incentives. Since it effectively reduced the cost of finance to non-taxpaying firms it may have stimulated investment. By raising the level of investment in recessionary periods when conditions of declining profitability might be expected to be encountered, leasing may also act in a counter-cyclical manner by allowing investment to be brought forward.

The gains from this change in timing may be very important to the economy both in counteracting the effects of the traditional trade cycle and in counteracting some of the factors of recent tight monetary policy most harmful to economic growth. In the first case, the appropriate timing for investment expenditure by firms during the trade cycle is largely in the period of recession so that they might respond rapidly to a recovery of demand. However, this is just when investment is the most difficult to finance because profits are low and cash flow is strained. Leasing, on the one hand, has relatively small demands on cash flow in the short run and, on the other, enables firms which still have taxable capacity to use it for the benefit of those that do not (and, of course, to increase their own profitable activity). Without those benefits of retiming there is the recurrent problem, when trade cycles are of short duration, that investment financed during the upturn comes on stream too late, at a point when the market is turning down.

In the second case, a policy regime which has its main effect on economic behaviour through tight monetary control will tend to generate high real interest rates and exchange rates. The former will tend to discourage investment directly by making it more difficult to find projects which will offer an adequate, real rate of return. It will also influence it indirectly because of increased debt servicing costs, reduced profits and harm to the cash flow. Profits will also be affected through the pressures on competitiveness imposed by the high exchange rate (in a fixed exchange rate regime the monetary policy has to be accompanied by deflation to have the same effect). Here again, leasing offers a means of continuing to be able to acquire the use of new assets under more favourable cost and cash flow conditions than is the case for other forms of finance. Leasing may have improved the efficiency of capital markets by spreading the effects of capital allowances and providing a cheap form of finance which might not have been forthcoming from other sources.

Thus through a number of mechanisms leasing may have had a major impact on the investment behaviour of the firm and the economy as a whole. Our study has been centred on examining the hypotheses that through tax advantage leasing has increased the level of investment and changed its timing in relation to fluctuations in the general level of economic activity.

## 1.6   THE STRUCTURE OF THE PROJECT

The project therefore included an investigation of the manner in which the rapid expansion of leasing affected investment behaviour, particularly in manufacturing industry. It also examined whether leasing affected the quantity and timing of investment at the macroeconomic level and how this relates to growth and cyclical fluctuations in the economy. An important part of the study has been the consideration of the significance of tax investment incentives on leasing and to contrast the effectiveness of these incentives with other incentives to invest. Data have been drawn from official sources[10] and the Equipment Leasing Association's annual surveys of the leasing activities of its members. This has been supplemented by a survey of lessors conducted by structured interviews and a postal questionnaire survey of lessees. In addition to examining the evidence in the UK, comparisons have been made with experience in other countries, where institutional arrangements and conditions are very different, based on information provided by various national leasing organisations and personal interviews. As well as considering the effects of leasing from a historical perspective, the project has sought to assess the likely effects on investment in the future, especially in view of the recent changes in the tax structure contained in the 1984 Finance Act.

# 2 The Growth of Leasing in the UK

## 2.1 EARLY HISTORY

Although the rapid growth in equipment leasing experienced in the UK during the 1970s and early 1980s is a relatively recent phenomenon, the use of leasing to finance the aquisition of capital assets has its immediate origins in the nineteenth century. Clark has identified the growth of the railway system as the principal instrument in developing leasing as a source of industrial finance.[1] A shortage of capital to finance the purchase of railway wagons arose by the mid nineteenth century as a result of the expansion in industrialisation, particularly the demand for coal, and the replacement of other forms of transport by the railways. In response railway wagon leasing companies were formed. Interestingly, one such company, The North Central Wagon Company, which in 1971 merged with Lombard Banking to form Lombard North Central, has survived to the present day. Despite the fact that leasing was largely replaced by hire purchase type agreements in the latter part of the nineteenth century, the financing of railway wagons through leasing was an important formative influence on future patterns of business finance in the UK.

However, although its origins are to be found in nineteenth-century industrialisation and its use continued subsequently, the real growth of equipment leasing as it is understood today began in the early 1960s. In the post-war period there was a considerable growth in consumer finance and in the number of firms offering such facilities. By the late 1950s, as a consequence of increasing regulation of the consumer market, rising competition and availability of funds, a number of finance houses became interested in developing the business credit side of their activities. Leasing had developed significantly both as a method of finance and a sales-aid during the 1950s in the USA and it was felt that similar opportunities might exist in the UK. Following earlier discussions in the USA, 1960 saw the formation of the Mercantile Leasing Company in the UK jointly owned by Mercantile Credit and the United States Leasing Corporation.[2] The incorporation of this company can be said to have marked the beginning of modern equipment leasing on a large scale in this country. Other finance houses and merchant banks soon followed Mercantile Credit into the leasing market.

There are, unfortunately, no detailed data on the early growth of leasing in the UK. The Equipment Leasing Association's series on assets acquired by its members for finance leasing does not commence until 1971 and the Department of Trade and Industry quarterly inquiry into leasing began in 1975. However, observers have suggested that initial growth was 'steady' during the early 1960s.[3] Leasing was offered as an alternative method of finance on the basis of certain advantages, namely, that it was capital saving, conserved other sources of credit, and made budgeting easier. It was initially marketed to large companies with high credit rating because, unlike hire purchase, no deposit was required.

Growth from the mid 1960s showed an upward trend (as indicated in Table 2.1).[4]

*Table* 2.1   Growth of leasing by finance and accepting houses 1965–9

| Year | Book value of equipment leased at year-end | | |
| | *Finance houses* £m | *Accepting houses* £m | *Total* £m |
| --- | --- | --- | --- |
| 1965 | 50 | 6 | 56 |
| 1966 | 52 | 9 | 61 |
| 1967 | 64 | 18 | 82 |
| 1968 | 95 | 26 | 121 |
| 1969 | 127 | 38 | 165 |

*Source*:   Finance Houses and *Board of Trade Journal*.

A number of factors influenced growth during this period. Leasing became gradually more accepted as prejudice in favour of the ownership of assets diminished and the advantages of leasing became known. Of particular importance was the off balance sheet nature of leasing and the avoidance of capital expenditure controls.

Growth in the use of computers and computer leasing was also a significant factor in stimulating the development of the leasing market. Computers were marketed predominantly under operating lease agreements which enabled users to avoid the risk of technological obsolescence. Computer leasing was influential in disseminating knowledge of leasing both as a method of finance and a marketing tool.

Monetary policy in the form of credit controls from the mid 1960s onwards may have restrained the growth of leasing, but in 1969 the Bank of England partially relaxed restrictions by consenting that some lending by finance houses and banks to separate leasing subsidiaries and associated companies would not be included in credit limits. A change in monetary policy came with the introduction of Competition and Credit Control in September 1971. This not only removed the necessity of such exemptions but, more importantly, stimulated the major clearing banks to expand their leasing activities through wholly owned subsidiary companies. Without this increased involvement by the clearing banks it is unlikely that leasing would have grown so rapidly in the following years.

## 2.2   THE EFFECTS OF TAX ALLOWANCES

During the 1960s tax considerations were of no significance to the expansion of leasing. Capital allowances in this period, although subject to a number of changes, remained at relatively low levels and were replaced in 1966 by direct investment grants. Table 2.2 shows the types and rates of investment incentives available during this period.

Tax advantages developed during the early 1970s and were a major

*Table* 2.2   Grants and allowances for plant and machinery 1959–84

| Announcement date | Investment allowances % | Initial allowances % | Grants % |
|---|---|---|---|
| 7–4–59 | 20 | 10 | |
| 5–11–62 | 30 | 10 | |
| 3–4–63 | 30 | 10 | |
| 17–1–66 | | | 20 |
| 1–12–66 | | | 25 |
| 1–1–69 | | | 20 |
| | First-year allowances % | | |
| 27–10–70 | 60 | | |
| 19–7–71 | 80 | | |
| 21–3–72 | 100 | | |

*Source*:   Adapted from Mellis and Richardson (1976) table 2, p. 32.

influence in stimulating rapid growth. Table 2.3 shows the growth in assets acquired (at cost) by members of the Equipment Leasing Association for finance leasing. These figures have not been adjusted for changes in membership.

*Table* 2.3    Assets acquired (at cost) by members of the Equipment Leasing Association for finance leasing (pounds million at current prices)

| 1971 | 159 | 1976 | 421 | 1981 | 2674 |
|------|-----|------|------|------|------|
| 1972 | 130 | 1977 | 675 | 1982 | 2834 |
| 1973 | 280 | 1978 | 1214 | 1983 | 2894 |
| 1974 | 321 | 1979 | 1802 | 1984 | 4012 |
| 1975 | 340 | 1980 | 2359 | 1985 | 5757 |

*Source*:    Equipment Leasing Association.

It has been shown that in theory market imperfections provide a rationale for leasing, especially when lessors still have taxable capacity and lessees are tax exhausted.[5] During the 1970s the combination of worsening economic conditions and changes in the system of corporation tax gave rise to such a situation. Early in the decade a number of adjustments were made to the fiscal structure with the objective of stimulating investment and alleviating the impact of inflation. In October 1970, it was announced that investment grants, which had been criticised because they were costly to administer and had benefited both profitable and unprofitable firms, were to be replaced by first-year capital allowances. In the case of plant and machinery, the capital allowance introduced enabled the firm to offset 60 per cent of the cost of an asset against taxable profit. This was raised to 80 per cent in July 1971 and to 100 per cent in March 1972.[6] Stock appreciation allowances were introduced in 1975 to compensate for inflation-induced increases in the value of physical stocks held by firms.

However, these changes, together with inflationary pressure and rising interest rates during the period, did not have the same effect on all sectors of the economy. The expansion of capital allowances and tax reliefs in conjunction with other existing reliefs, such as tax deductability of loan interest, and declining profitability severely affected the tax position of many non-financial firms. Indeed, a relatively large number of firms, mainly those in manufacturing industries which tended to have large capital expenditure programmes, experienced tax exhaustion where available allowances were greater than taxable profits. With provisions available within the tax structure for carrying forward unused allowances, not only were relatively large numbers of firms not paying tax but they were likely to remain so well into the future. A 1982 Green Paper on Corporation Tax estimated that in the late 1970s only about 40 per cent of all companies were earning sufficient profits (after tax reliefs and allowances) to pay mainstream corporation tax.[7]

The position of firms in the financial sector was very different. Inflation and relatively high rates of interest had aided the profitability of financial institutions, especially that of the major clearing banks. Unlike non-financial firms they undertook comparatively little direct capital expenditure and since they did not hold much in the way of physical stocks, were unable to use up all the tax reliefs and allowances available. With this imbalance in the taxpaying position of firms in the financial and non-financial sectors of the economy, there was a strong incentive to lease. The lessor as legal owner could claim capital allowances and offset these against taxable profits or the taxable profits of a parent company.[8] The latter concept of 'group relief' was particularly important in the case of the clearing banks which were faced with potentially large tax liabilities during the period.[9] The benefit from tax deferral reduced the return required by the lessor on financing investment in leased assets. This was passed on in part to the lessee as reduced rental payments. The supply of funds for leasing was therefore largely determined by the taxable capacity of lessors. Through leasing, the lessor gained by deferring taxation and the non-taxpaying lessee obtained a major proportion of the benefit of capital allowances[10] in the form of asset finance that was often effectively cheaper than other market rates of interest. Periods of inflation and relatively high nominal rates of interest increased this differential.

Furthermore, lessors have been able to offer very attractive rates near the end of their financial year because the time lapse in receiving capital allowances is less than that for leases transacted earlier in the year. Ignoring the complication of Advanced Corporation Tax payments, while capital allowances are accumulated during the year they only have their impact on tax payments when tax is due. Thus capital expenditure undertaken near the end of the company financial year will have a shorter period before the offsetting effect on the company's cash flow in the form of reduction in tax payments occurs. Hence, from the point of view of a group of companies, bunching capital expenditure at the end of each subsidiary's financial year helps

*Table* 2.4    Leasing rates and Finance Houses Association base rate 1977–85

| | Average leasing rate[1] (%) | Average Finance Houses Association base rate[2] (%) |
|---|---|---|
| 1977 | 8.1 | 9.4 |
| 1978 | 9.1 | 8.8 |
| 1979 | 8.8 | 13.4 |
| 1980 | 9.9 | 16.9 |
| 1981 | 9.6 | 14.2 |
| 1982 | 9.8 | 13.3 |
| 1983 | 9.5 | 10.5 |
| 1984 | 6.2 | 10.8 |
| 1985 | 9.7 | 11.2 |

[1] Calculated using the monthly average leasing rate for five-year leases with quarterly rentals. The equivalent interest rate for lease rentals assumes the lessee to be permanently non-taxpaying.
[2] Calculated using the Finance Houses Association base rate prevailing during each month.
*Sources*:    Saturn Lease Underwriting Limited and *Financial Statistics*.

to minimise the time before the offset takes place. Since the capital assets are for leasing it is irrelevant, in terms of actually producing physical goods or services with the asset, which subsidiary actually undertakes the investment expenditure. The choice can be made by the lessor merely on the basis of the maximum financial gain to the lessor group. A number of large lessors have therefore specifically formed subsidiary companies with different financial years to take maximum advantage of this 'year end effect'.

An indication of the relative position of leasing rates over the period 1977 to 1985 is given in Table 2.4, although the figures can only be regarded as a very broad approximation as leasing rates can vary considerably according to the nature of the transaction and the position of lessor and lessee. The Finance Houses Association Base Rate shown in the table is not, however, the rate at which lending by finance houses actually takes place. That rate will normally be at a margin over the base rate. Thus the table will tend to understate the differential in favour of leasing.

It is evident from earlier descriptions of the two major forms of leasing – finance and operating – that tax advantages of leasing are more important in finance leasing than operating leasing. Finance

*Table* 2.5    Expenditure on fixed assets for leasing 1975–85 (pounds million)

| | *Operational leasing and finance leasing* *Hiring (Class 84 SIC 80)* | | | |
|---|---|---|---|---|
| | *Current prices* | *Constant (1980) prices* | *Current prices* | *Constant (1980) prices* |
| 1975 | 305 | 445 | 320 | 561 |
| 1976 | 340 | 447 | 434 | 665 |
| 1977 | 494 | 575 | 633 | 821 |
| 1978 | 544 | 607 | 1146 | 1405 |
| 1979 | 681 | 714 | 1734 | 1933 |
| 1980 | 719 | 719 | 2158 | 2158 |
| 1981 | 958 | 927 | 2240 | 2079 |
| 1982 | 1028 | 967 | 2700 | 2374 |
| 1983 | 1239 | 1170 | 2483 | 2124 |
| 1984 | 1162 | 1057 | 3516 | 2879 |
| 1985 | 1261 | 1092 | 4887 | 3772 |

*Source*:    Business Statistics Office.

leasing has formed the largest part of the overall leasing market as is shown in Table 2.5.

The figures show clearly that while the overall trend in finance leasing has been upward, growth in real terms has been spasmodic, with strong growth in the late 1970s but downturns in 1981 and 1983. Operating leasing has also shown variation in the rate of annual growth.

## 2.3    OTHER CAUSES OF GROWTH

Although tax considerations have been a key factor in the rapid growth of leasing, there is evidence to suggest that the increased demand for this type of facility was not totally tax based.[11] Other, non-tax, reasons include the fact that leasing allows the firm to avoid having to make the large lump sum payments that are usually found in capital expenditure. This is particularly important in periods when firms are short of cash. As was mentioned in Chapter 1, since firms have been able to keep assets 'acquired' through leasing off the balance sheet, it is in effect possible for the firm to have a higher borrowing (or 'debt capacity'). The simple convenience and flexibility of leasing from the point of view of the lessee has been influential in stimulating growth. The attractiveness of leasing in the 1970s was also aided by the lack of medium-term fixed finance available from financial institutions.

In addition to these factors, leasing tended to be marketed in a different manner from other forms of finance. Leasing facilities were often made available through a direct sales force rather than through traditional banking links and offices.

Tax advantages have tended to differ in significance in specific areas of the market. It is common in the leasing industry to divide the total market according to the size of the leasing transaction. Following terminology used in the USA, leases are categorised into small, medium and big 'ticket' leases according to monetary values. Divisions of this kind are by their very nature arbitrary but the common practice is to apply the terms as follows:

— 'small ticket' of less than £25 000 size of agreement
— 'medium ticket' leasing from £25 000 to £5 million
— 'big ticket' over £5 million

Small ticket sales-aid leasing has grown largely independent of tax advantage. Lessors have found this type of business to be profitable in its own right[12] and lessees have been motivated by service and convenience. Tax advantage has been most important in medium to big ticket finance leasing where the decision to lease is often influenced by cost factors alone.

## 2.4   DISTRIBUTION BY TYPE OF ASSET

The leasing of plant and machinery has formed a major part of the market during its expansion. Table 2.6 shows an analysis of the finance leasing business of members of the Equipment Leasing Association broken down by type of asset over the period 1976 to 1984.

A point of particular interest is the rapid growth of car leasing. The upsurge of car leasing in 1977 resulted from the abolition in June of that year of hiring controls (which had required the payment of forty-two weeks rentals in advance) over cars for business purposes, and the ruling of the Special Commissioners that lessors were eligible for 100 per cent first-year capital allowances. However, the Budget of June 1979 introduced a measure which limited the 100 per cent first-year allowance to cars for short-term hire, taxis and private cars.

*Table* 2.6   Finance leasing business of Equipment Leasing Association members by type of asset 1976–84 (£m at current prices; % share in parentheses)

| Assets acquired during year (at cost) | 1976 | 1977 | 1978 | 1979 | 1980 | 1981 | 1982 | 1983 | 1984 |
|---|---|---|---|---|---|---|---|---|---|
| Plant and machinery | 139 | 198 | 250 | 415 | 712 | 801 | 957 | 1125 | 1524 |
| | (33) | (29) | (20) | (23) | (32) | (38) | (35) | (39) | (38) |
| Computer and office equipment | 78 | 164 | 240 | 315 | 445 | 380 | 477 | 702 | 835 |
| | (19) | (24) | (20) | (17) | (20) | (18) | (18) | (25) | (21) |
| Ships and aircraft[1] | 117 | 108 | 158 | 298 | 342 | 355 | 517 | 236 | 551 |
| | (28) | (16) | (13) | (17) | (15) | (17) | (19) | (8) | (14) |
| Commercial vehicles | 58 | 114 | 154 | 225 | 291 | 225 | 320 | 324 | 450 |
| | (14) | (17) | (13) | (12) | (13) | (11) | (12) | (11) | (11) |
| Cars | 6 | 57 | 343 | 468 | 267 | 222 | 256 | 296 | 338 |
| | (1) | (9) | (28) | (26) | (12) | (11) | (9) | (10) | (8) |
| Industrial buildings | | | | | | 27 | 95 | 61 | 54 |
| | | | | | | (1) | (3) | (2) | (1) |
| Other[2] | 23 | 34 | 69 | 81 | 169 | 92 | 118 | 150 | 260 |
| | (5) | (5) | (6) | (5) | (8) | (4) | (4) | (5) | (7) |
| | 421 | 675 | 1214 | 1802 | 2226 | 2102 | 2740 | 2894 | 4012 |
| | (100) | (100) | (100) | (100) | (100) | (100) | (100) | (100) | (100) |
| International leasing | | | | | 133 | 572 | 94 | | |
| | 421 | 675 | 1214 | 1802 | 2359 | 2674 | 2834 | 2894 | 4012 |

[1] Includes oil exploration and production equipment from 1980.
[2] Includes railway rolling stock, shop fittings and agricultural equipment.
*Source*:   Equipment Leasing Association.

All others were subject to a 25 per cent writing down allowance. This change is reflected in the subsequent statistics but, nevertheless, car leasing has remained an important part of the Equipment Leasing Association's members business.

## 2.5   SECTORAL DISTRIBUTION

Looking at the way leasing has developed in terms of the sectors to which assets have been leased rather than the distribution of the assets themselves, Table 2.7 shows analysis of the finance leasing business of members of the Equipment Leasing Association broken down by type of lessee over the period 1977 to 1983. The importance of the manufacturing sector in leasing is clear. On average, manufacturing has accounted for approximately 30 per cent of the finance leasing business of Equipment Leasing Association members. It is also apparent that in recent years there has been an increase in assets leased to distributive and other service industries. Neither the need to invest in large projects nor the problems of tax exhaustion are confined to manufacturing particularly with the rise of automation.

Leasing to central and local government and international leasing have both been affected by changes in the regulations governing the eligibility of leased assets for first-year capital allowances. These changes in part account for the decline in business in both areas after their peak in 1981. The 1980 Finance Act replaced the 100 per cent first-year allowance with a 25 per cent writing down allowance for assets leased to non-taxpaying bodies. The Act made a distinction between statutorily taxpaying bodies, such as nationalised industries, passenger transport executives or private water authorities, and non-taxpaying bodies such as local authorities or the health services. The reduction in allowance also applied to non-residents outside the UK.

There was no immediate downturn in leasing to central and local government after the legislation. Clearly one would not expect leasing to disappear in this area because even with a 25 per cent writing down allowance there is still some tax advantage. There are, however, other factors acting in favour of leasing in this sector. One is simply that it can be possible to circumvent capital expenditure controls in some authorities either by treating leasing as a current item or by merely reducing the size of payment needed initially. However, although, with the exception of Scotland, equipment leasing does not normally form part of the capital allocation for each authority, central government does include an estimate for overall leasing by local authorities in drawing up allocations. Public sector budgeting normally attributes the entire capital expenditure to the purchasing department in the first year. Certainly the market is attractive from the perspective of the lessor because of the relatively large amounts of business that can be transacted with comparatively little risk.

The picture shown in Table 2.7 for international leasing is misleading as it was only separately recorded from 1980. Hence there was no sudden emergence from a zero base in 1980, merely growth from an unknown previous value. Despite the fall in initial allowances from 100 per cent to 25 per cent as a result of the 1980 Finance Act, there was an increase from 1980 to 1981. However, this was followed by a

*Table* 2.7   Finance leasing business of equipment leasing (£m at current prices; % share in parentheses)

| Assets acquired during year (at cost) | 1977 | 1978 | 1979 | 1980 | 1981 | 1982 | 1983 |
|---|---|---|---|---|---|---|---|
| Manufacturers | 215 | 363 | 571 | 642 | 711 | 897 | 970 |
| | (32) | (30) | (32) | (29) | (34) | (33) | (34) |
| Other industrial | 119 | 166 | 256 | 208 | 273 | 391 | 476 |
| | (18) | (14) | (14) | (9) | (13) | (14) | (16) |
| Transport | 135 | 285 | 377 | 435 | 176 | 360 | 292 |
| | (20) | (23) | (21) | (20) | (8) | (13) | (10) |
| Agricultural | 27 | 33 | 68 | 70 | 99 | 168 | 171 |
| | (4) | (3) | (4) | (3) | (5) | (6) | (6) |
| Distributive and other service industries | 98 | 267 | 434 | 670 | 589 | 724 | 792 |
| | (14) | (22) | (24) | (30) | (28) | (27) | (27) |
| Central and local government | 81 | 100 | 96 | 201 | 254 | 200 | 193 |
| | (12) | (8) | (5) | (9) | (12) | (7) | (7) |
| | 675 | 1214 | 1802 | 2226 | 2102 | 2740 | 2894 |
| | (100) | (100) | (100) | (100) | (100) | (100) | (100) |
| International leasing | | | | 133 | 572 | 94 | |
| | 675 | 1214 | 1802 | 2359 | 2674 | 2834 | 2894 |

*Source*:   Equipment Leasing Association.

marked decrease in the next year reflecting the effects of the 1982 Finance Act which further reduced the 25 per cent writing down allowance on assets leased to non-residents to 10 per cent.

## 2.6   THE 1984 FINANCE ACT

The significance of tax advantages and consequent effects on leasing rates and investment have been demonstrated by the effects of the 1984 Finance Act. The main provisions, announced in the 1984 Budget, relating to changes in capital allowances for plant and machinery and tax rates are shown in Table 2.8.

The 1984 Budget proposed that the 100 per cent first-year allowance for plant and machinery should be phased out leaving a 25 per cent writing down allowance by 1986. The rate of corporation tax was also to be reduced in annual steps to 35 per cent. These changes subsequently came into effect. However, behaviour in the leasing

*Table* 2.8   Changes to the system of Corporation Tax announced in the 1984
             budget

| Financial year[1] | Corporation Tax rate[2] | First-year allowances[3] |
|---|---|---|
| 1983 | 50% | 100% (a) |
| 1984 | 45% | 75% (b) |
| 1985 | 40% | 50% (c) |
| 1986 | 35% | NIL (d) |
| Stock relief abolished from 13 March 1984 | | |

[1] Year ending 31 March of following year.
[2] Main rate (previously 52%) – small companies rate reduced from 38% to
30% for financial year 1983 and subsequent years.
[3] First-year capital allowances for plant and machinery – other allowances
will be adjusted during the transitional period.
  (a) expenditure before 14 March 1984
  (b) expenditure on or after 14 March 1984
  (c) expenditure on or after 1 April 1985
  (d) expenditure on or after 1 April 1986 – 25% writing down allowance
      (reducing balance)
*Source*:   Treasury.


market will have been affected both by the actual changes when they
happened and by expectations of whether the sequence of changes
would occur as originally planned. These changes in the corporation
tax structure clearly had most serious implications for leasing and
their impact is still being felt. The short-term effect during the
transitional period was to engender a substantial boom in leasing.
This upturn is illustrated in the Equipment Leasing Association data
and official data in Tables 2.3 and 2.5.

The increase in finance leasing activity was in part stimulated by
the lowering of leasing rates brought about by the tax and allowance
changes in the transitional period. The reduction of capital allowances alone without altering the rate of corporation tax would have
led to an increase in leasing rates but this was offset by the reduction
in tax rates. Capital allowances are received relatively early in the
lease whereas rental income is taxed later at a lower rate. A tax
saving has therefore resulted which has been passed on to the lessee
in the form of lower rentals. This compensatory effect applied until
the end of March 1985. Rates since then have tended to move
upwards as the effects of the changes have been felt but have
generally remained below the levels of alternative methods of
finance. Leasing was also stimulated in the short run simply by the

knowledge that the terms would be less favourable in subsequent years. Hence, where possible, it could be advantageous to advance the timing of investment decisions. The extent of this retiming is shown by the enormous bunching of leasing in the last quarter of each of the transitional financial years. Lessors have been able to accomodate the increase in leasing activity because, as a consequence of lower capital allowances, the total level of business that can be conducted before taxable profits are exhausted has risen.

The future of leasing in the UK following the full implementation of the 1984 Finance Act is dealt with in a later chapter.

(bl)

# 3 Leasing from the Viewpoint of the Lessor

The existence of a leasing contract results from the conclusion of a bargain between lessor and lessee. Both parties contribute to the striking of the bargain. Although for small contracts the lessee may in effect be only able to take up an offer under standard terms and conditions it is not purely his decision-making alone which determines whether the contract takes place. The lessor has to decide upon the terms and upon the amount of business he wishes to transact. Furthermore, if leasing is only one part of the financial services the lessor offers he has to make decisions on the balance of his business and the relative profitability of it.

Simply put, there is an important supply side in the determination of the amount and cost of leasing, not just a demand side. Thus although previous analysis has focused primarily on the decision of the lessee in determining the effects on the size and timing of investment, it is equally important to consider the behaviour of lessors as in a very real sense they make the market.

However, two further considerations directed our research towards looking at lessors before looking at lessees. The first is simply that there are fewer lessors than there are lessees and it is possible to survey a large proportion of the industry individually and hence build up a comprehensive picture of their activity. The second is that lessors deal with many lessees. They are therefore likely to be aware, from a wide range of clients, what factors are prevalent in motivating lessees. Thus approaching lessors gives information not just on lessor behaviour but also on that of lessees as well.

Not surprisingly, lessors are much better informed about the technicalities of the operation of the leasing market and the ways in which it has developed in the past, and could develop further in the future, than are lessees in general. Hence, a survey lessors appeared the sensible place to start the research.

Thus although the primary objective of this study is to determine the possible effects of the growth of leasing on investment in the economy, the initial research strategy was to conduct a survey of lessors with the aim of collecting data not only on characteristics of the leasing market but also on lessors' perceptions of lessee behaviour.

Considerable attention was given to the identification of effects of leasing on investment and the manner in which these were brought about. While this approach was largely qualitative it formed the basis of the more detailed analysis which followed.

The survey of lessors involved structured interviews at two organisational levels. Firstly, after gaining approval from their head offices, leasing companies were approached at branch or regional office level with the express objective of conducting interviews with 'field' personnel engaged principally in small to medium-sized leasing transactions. A sample of companies operating in the South West Economic Planning Region was selected for this purpose. Secondly, interviews were arranged with senior personnel of major leasing companies, generally involved in policy decisions and large lease negotiations, at head office level. In the event this distinction in organisational levels did not strictly hold as some companies which were requested to take part in the 'South West Survey' were willing only to participate at head office level. However, for ease of exposition the summary has been divided into two sections – the 'South West Survey' (including those companies who cooperated only at a senior level) and the 'Major Lessor Survey' which covers those interviews conducted at the head offices of major leasing companies.

## 3.1 THE 'SOUTH WEST' SURVEY

### 3.1.1 The Sample

The survey consisted of a number of structured interviews with lessors carried out during January and February 1985. Each interview covered the same topics with standard questions which the respondents were allowed to answer freely. In some sections, however, predesigned prompts (check-lists) were used when it was felt that areas which could be of particular relevance might have been omitted. The questions were intentionally wide ranging and included not only an examination of lessor practice but also lessee behaviour as perceived by the respondents.

A sample of twenty leasing companies known to have offices in the South-West was drawn from lessors operating in the UK. Of the twenty companies sixteen were members of the Equipment Leasing Association. Sixteen of the twenty companies agreed to participate and fourteen of these were interviewed. Of the remaining six, four were found to be largely irrelevant to the study as they did little or no leasing in the South West and in only two cases was it not possible to arrange a convenient interview. Thus although the selection method was somewhat biased, the survey covered firms conducting a major proportion of the leasing business in the South West. Five interviews took place in London and one by telephone rather than face to face.

Although by necessity the sample drawn for this type of in-depth survey is small, the respondents represented quite a broad spectrum of the leasing industry. Lessors ranged from those dealing in relatively small items of capital equipment, such as typewriters or vending machines, to those prepared to lease major plant and machinery. Those lessors taking part in the survey had the following characteristics:

— All the leasing companies interviewed formed part of a company or group of companies.

— Two companies specialised in leasing only. Others offered additional facilities including hire purchase conditional sale, credit sale, personal and commercial loans, factoring, block discounting, invoice discounting car hire, stocking loans, venture capital and equity participation finance.

— Of the eight companies interviewed in the South West and giving data for that area, four were principally engaged in medium ticket leasing, three in small ticket leasing and one had its business roughly divided equally between small and medium ticket leasing.

— Of the five companies interviewed in the London area and giving data of a more generalised nature, one operated throughout the market, one was principally engaged in large ticket leasing, two in medium/large ticket leasing and one in small ticket leasing.

— The company interviewed by telephone was largely engaged in small ticket leasing.

— All the companies interviewed were predominantly finance lessors with the exception of one where most of its activity was operating leasing.

In the analysis of the structured interviews, therefore, care has been taken to relate comments and observations made by lessors to whether the respondent is a specialist or diversified company; to whether it operates in a particular sector of the market; to whether regional factors may be applicable; and to whether finance or operating leasing forms the major part of its business.

### 3.2.1 What Assets Are Suitable for Leasing

Leasing's contribution to the economy would be reduced if only some assets were leasable. Indeed, since it has offered more attractive terms than other forms of financing, this might result in a distortion in the pattern of investment. However, it appears, from the lessors point of view, that almost any type of capital asset can be leased. This does not of course mean that they are all equally suitable. Among those specifically mentioned by lessors were agricultural equipment, commercial vehicles, cars, office equipment, vending machines, catering equipment, printing presses, computers, wholesale/retail shop equipment, machine tools, computer numerically controlled equipment, production lines, leisure equipment, and aircraft.

On the other hand, lessors indicated that they would avoid:

— equipment to which the legal title may be in doubt (e.g. fixtures and fittings attached to buildings).

— equipment on which capital allowances may not be claimed.

— equipment which is specialised or depreciates in value rapidly so that the residual value is at risk.

— equipment which is subject to large third party risks.

— equipment provided by 'dubious' suppliers.

It is interesting to note that assets regarded as high risk varied somewhat between lessors. For example, some were prepared to lease computers whilst others avoided them, considering the residual value to be questionable. Other assets specifically mentioned by lessors as being unattractive included films, containers, fork-lift trucks, televisions, jukeboxes, cash tills, photocopiers and foreign investment.

The following general characteristics were considered by lessors as desirable in assets to be leased. They should be:

— non-specialised,
— identifiable (by serial numbers or plates),

— mobile/portable/de-mountable/not attached to a building/easy to repossess,
— non-consumable/maintain a residual value/have a ready market/ have a useful life in excess of the lease period.

All of these characteristics relate primarily to the security value of the asset but almost without exception lessors were eager to point out that, although security was important, it is the creditworthiness of the client that is most significant in the leasing transaction. Thus a 'blue chip' company may be able to lease assets which are basically high risk whereas a company without an established 'track record' would find it extremely difficult if not impossible to do so. One lessor suggested that the underwriting of a lease was more stringent than that of other forms of finance and was a question of drawing an appropriate balance between the quality of the asset, the quality of the supplier and most importantly the quality of the client. This balance was reflected in the resultant leasing terms offered to the lessee.

It is therefore clear that leasing could have an effect on the pattern of investment. We should also emphasise that we are only considering leasing of plant, equipment and vehicles, not buildings. Leasing has grown in that area as well as in the company sector. However, the size of the possible distortion may vary with the creditworthiness of the lessee. Hence, since creditworthiness also varies over time particularly with the economic cycle, there could be fluctuations in the impact on the pattern of investment.

### 3.1.3 Variables Affecting the Method of Financing Capital Investment by Firms

Although the use of leasing is very widespread, we wondered whether there were certain types of firm that had found it more attractive. Since there are no data on which to analyse this question we specifically addressed it to lessors to see if they had noticed any particular trends. We only attempted to identify broad structural characteristics relating to companies that used leasing as a method of funding capital expenditure. However, it was felt by most lessors that close correlations did not exist between leasing and factors such as the size of the firm or the industry it was in. Leasing tended to be employed throughout the market. Indeed, one lessor felt that the choice of leasing as a funding option was specific to each occasion and hence it was difficult therefore to think in terms of any precise characteristics of firms *per se* which could be associated with leasing. Taking the views of the whole sample of lessors, the following general observations can be derived:

## (a)   Size

The size of firm was not usually regarded as a particularly important factor, although large firms may lease because they tend to have a higher level of sophistication in their financial policy or simply because their capital expenditure budgets are large. On the other hand, small firms may turn to leasing because they lack a range of alternatives or because they do not regard leasing as debt. The lessors observed that their clients were distributed across the whole range of company size.

## (b)   Type of Industry

There was no close relationship identified between the type of industry and the use of leasing although many lessors observed that, of course, capital-intensive industries tend to show a higher level of leasing than others, but not necessarily in proportion to the level of their investment. Generally, it was considered that leasing was used by a large number of quite diverse industries.

## (c)   Products

Particular products, on the other hand, were thought to be identified with leasing. For example, sales-aid leasing is clearly a marketing device which is fairly widespread, especially in areas such as vehicle sales and office equipment. Photocopiers were singled out as an example of a product which is rarely 'sold' in any other manner.

## (d)   Rate of Growth of the Firm

Most of the lessors interviewed considered the rate of growth of the firm to be of importance and two reasons were identified. First, growing companies tended to have relatively large investment requirements as a result of expansion. Second, as a consequence of rapid development, firms may experience cash flow difficulties which may be eased by leasing because, on the one hand, it may provide an additional source of finance and, on the other, it avoids having to make a large capital outlay on the assets at the beginning of the period. This, therefore, means that leasing tends to play a more than proportionately important role in the expansion of the economy. A point which directly contradicts some of the intentions of the 1984 Finance Act.

## (e)   Profitability

As might be expected, lessors identified the profitability of firms as an item affecting the decision to lease (this was mentioned especially by lessors operating in the medium ticket market) but the reasons given for the importance of this factor varied. Some linked this to the advantages of tax-exhausted companies in leasing; others to a lack of internally generated funds. However, lessors were anxious to point out that they were not interested in supporting ailing companies but in assisting where there was a logical and sound financial reason. In addition, it was observed that it would be wrong to give the impression that leasing was limited to 'non-profitable' companies. One lessor indicated that a number of major companies with substantial profits had used leasing. Such companies leased assets for reasons which were not necessarily tax based or linked to a limitation of funding operations.

This distinction of the medium ticket category from the general run of leasing will therefore have an important role to play in mapping out the likely future when we consider the impact of the 1984 Finance Act, which in effect reduced the importance of a lack of profits in encouraging leasing. While small ticket and large ticket deals may have characteristics which sustain them, this may account for expectations that it is the medium range which will be hardest hit.

## (f)   Gearing

If leasing is a residual form of finance for investment, one might expect a positive relation between gearing and the use of leasing. However, lessors' opinions on the significance of the gearing of a firm were divided. Some lessors felt that gearing would vary from industry to industry and therefore would not be particularly important in aggregate. Others felt that whilst high gearing might be a reason for leasing from the lessee's point of view, they as lessors would not want to write business with a highly geared company unless there was an acceptable explanation why this was the case. Thus the general opinion was that the relationship between gearing and leasing was not very strong.

*(g)   Assets*

We discussed the range of assets lessors regarded as suitable for leasing earlier in this chapter, but it was also reported that some lessees appeared to have explicit policies to lease certain types of asset such as cars or items of office equipment. In these cases, leasing could be viewed as the 'norm' and hence not subject to explicit comparison with other methods of finance on each occasion. In these cases, when the relative attractiveness of leasing changes we can expect relatively little impact on the volume of leasing. A second characteristic of the assets picked by lessors was in areas where the depreciation of the asset is relatively rapid. Here, use of leasing enables the company to treat it as a revenue expense.

*(h)   Other Factors*

Lessors also mentioned several other less important factors including:

  (i) companies with fixed contracts tend to lease where a specific asset is required for a given period and budget considerations are important;
 (ii) subsidiary companies of US (and other foreign) based parents were well known for leasing because it could improve the apparent return on capital and circumvent capital budget constraints;
(iii) accountants particularly in favour of leasing in certain localities may stimulate leasing in an area.

### 3.1.4   Reasons for Leasing

The last two sections reflect our attempt to add to information available on the nature of leasing. However, we also thought it worthwhile to obtain lessors' views on why lessees make the decision to lease both, because from what is often a more experienced viewpoint they may be able to spot tendencies which no individual lessee can, and also because people's perceptions of the motivation for their own actions may be flawed. They may provide ex-post rationalisations or not be able to express it well. Lessors gave two main reasons why, in their view, lessees decide to lease: first, the tax advantages of leasing arising from capital allowances, and second, characteristics of leasing which lead to conservation of cash flow. However, within this general pattern tax advantages were not thought important for small ticket/sales-aid leasing and cash flow was not a principal reason for big ticket leasing. While the fact that leasing can provide 100 per cent finance was found to be important by some lessors, others felt that this was not a significant consideration in the sense that although the lessee was not required to provide any of the finance for the asset initially, in practice, particularly in high risk areas, up to six months rentals could be required in advance by the lessor.

A further issue raised was the fixed nature of leasing and consequent administrative ease and budgetary accuracy which was considered to be important in small and medium ticket leasing, where the overhead from funding other sources of finance could be very heavy in relation to the amount of funds required. The problem did not apply for big ticket deals where the overhead could be spread and fixed rates were held to be a distinct disadvantage.

Leasing as a hedge against inflation was generally regarded as having been a 'good selling point' in the past but was no longer quite so relevant as inflation rates fell. The ease with which a leasing agreement can be set up and its flexibility are important factors in the small/medium ticket sectors but one lessor indicated that this could apply to hire purchase as well (indeed the lessor in question considered leasing to require more careful underwriting than hire purchase). It is interesting that the same lessor observed that the fixed nature of leasing mentioned above applied equally to hire purchase. Thus while ease and flexibility may be a reason for leasing there must be further reasons which lead to it being selected in preference to hire purchase. Opinion was divided on whether leasing is a safeguard against rapid technological change and changing markets. This division often reflected the nature of the leasing business conducted by the lessor interviewed. The operating lessor taking part in the survey thought this reason important whilst many of the finance lessors pointed out that penalties could be quite severe for early termination of a contract, as the length of lease is geared to the useful life of the asset. One interesting exception was the respondent engaged in sales-aid/small ticket leasing who indicated that this was a very important aspect. Lessors also suggested that the easing of replacement decisions through leasing would be subject to the constraints of early termination penalties in the case of finance leasing.

Lessors tended to disagree on the importance of whether leasing provides an additional source of finance which preserves other lines of credit and whether this is a strong reason to lease. Some felt that lease finance and debt were substitutes whilst others felt that leasing might increase borrowing capacity largely due to a lack of disclosure in accounting information, which still persists. The possibility that leasing provides finance which may not be available from other sources was generally interpreted by lessors as 'last resort borrowing'. Whilst they felt that from time to time certain potential lessees might find this important, this type of business was to be avoided.

Not surprisingly, from the point of view of the lessor, there should be little difference in the creditworthiness of a company to take on a lease from that to take on any other financial liability. The timing of payments might have some effect at the margin because of the more viable projected cash flow, and the fact that leasing might be a smaller financial burden on the firm might also be a marginal consideration. Moreover, lessors expressed a dislike of business at the margin because of its higher risk. However, some did admit that in the early days of leasing, up to the mid 1970s, the creditworthiness of a company from the point of view of a lease had not always been viewed in the same light as that of other liabilities. This had two consequences. On the one hand, lease commitments may not always have been taken into account when assessing the appropriate level of lending to the firm. On the other, appraisal for lease finance may not always have taken into account the total financial position of the firm as it would for borrowing. It was considered by lessors that such anomalies had largely long since disappeared.

Leasing as part of a corporate plan was held to be most importance for larger, more sophisticated companies and was linked directly with tax planning and mitigation. Cost factors were considered to be related directly to the taxpaying position of the lessee and it was indicated that leasing rates have tended to vary in competitiveness through time, depending on the demand for leasing facilities and the amount of taxable capacity of lessors. It must be said that we were unable to collect enough data to test this hypothesis which is unfortunate as it is very significant in medium to big ticket finance leasing. It was also observed that leasing was most attractive in inflationary periods when interest rates were high.

These factors combined to indicate, not surprisingly, that despite the fact that much of the rise of leasing was due rather more to the increase in market penetration of a 'new' product, nevertheless, without the process of penetration, the use of leasing varied according to market conditions. In subsequent discussions we were not able to determine the extent to which competition squeezed margins when the market declined. One of the problems with making these assessments is that in some ways the leasing market moves in the opposite direction to other markets, while in others it moves with it. If credit is generally tight then the market for leasing will also be tight as lessees are looking for every possibility to obtain the use of the assets they wish to install, including leasing as well as finance of ownership. On the other hand, since leasing is affected by influences which do not apply to other forms of financing, pressure in the leasing market can occur because of improvements in its relative costs.

However, some of these distinct influences are related to general pressures. The tax advantage from leasing increases as profitability falls. Profitability is normally at its lowest in a recession. During the early part of a recession, at any rate, a major cause of that pressure may occur through monetary policy with a squeeze on credit through high interest rates or quantitative restrictions on the financial system, through special or supplementary deposits, for example. Thus, factors increasing demand and factors restricting supply may coincide. It is the inflation element which may make the major difference. Profitability of financial institutions is linked to nominal turnover rather than just real turnover and there is a tendency for relative profitability of financial institutions to increase in periods of high inflation, thus increasing the relative attractiveness of leasing to lessors.

While interest rates tend to rise in nominal terms during period of price inflation, the experience of the 1970s was that real rates of interest lagged and indeed were often negative. That, of course, would increase the demand for leasing. It is only when a credit squeeze and inflation coincide that demand for leasing is likely to be reduced. It is thus a complex matter to sort out these influences, particularly with the lack of data available, which was a major incentive for a pursuance of the surveys.

The fact that leasing involves no dilution of equity and reduces the risk of ownership was generally not regarded by lessors as an important reason to lease, and was felt by some respondents to be very much of a by-product rather than a primary motivation. The off-balance sheet characteristics of leasing were considered to be especially strong in big ticket leasing and in leasing to agriculture (one lessor described this as 'the number one reason' in agricultural leasing). Lessors in other sectors also found this to be important (and one suggested that this would continue despite the publication of SSAP 21). However, a number indicated that it was of significance in a historical context, but as the financial markets became more aware of leasing this had diminished. One lessor asserted that the majority of lessees do not capitalise leased assets and this was a significant factor in increasing borrowing capacity and improving the apparent return on capital (subsidiary companies were again mentioned in this context). These were clearly points we followed up with lessees, as is discussed in Chapter 4.

In addition to the formal reasons discussed above, a number of lessors pointed to the importance of marketing in leasing and that it had contributed significantly to its growth.

### 3.1.5 Leasing in the Decision-making Process of the Firm

We also asked lessors about their perception of the way lessees made the decision to use leasing, again as a means of acquiring indirect evidence. It was our belief that by observing the arguments lessees used and the nature of the case they put forward lessors might have a rather clearer view of the actual process of reasoning that lessees, as a group, went through. In particular, it might indicate where the real decision points lay by revealing the crucial parts in the discussion and indeed the person or group in the firm with whom the outstanding points were resolved.

We began by asking about the extent to which leasing appeared to be a simultaneous finance and investment decision and pursued the question at some length because this consideration is most important in examining the effects of leasing on the investment behaviour of firms. If leasing is thought to be a simultaneous finance and invest-ment decision then it may well have an effect over and above that of merely substituting one form of finance for another. If it is the case that the investment decision is made first and the financing decision second, then the fact that leasing is used by the firm is less likely to have an influence on that investment. Of course, when the terms of the lease proposal are determined the firm will appraise whether the investment is still warranted and, to the extent that leasing offers better terms, one would expect rejection to occur less frequently than for investment decisions as a whole. Indeed, the effect on investment may not be on the same transaction. The more favourable terms of the lease may enable the firm to undertake further investment pro-jects which would otherwise not have been thought financially viable. Nevertheless, if it were the case that the finance and investment decisions were taken together, then it would be rather easier to determine from lessees how much the existence of leasing affected the size and timing of their investment.

Lessors considered that the direct linking of leasing as a form of finance and the investment decision varied with the size of investment and the nature of the capital asset. Many held that in the medium ticket sector the decision to invest was made first. It appeared to them that major investment decisions were analysed completely by lessees, considering a wide range of variables including tax planning, whereas smaller investments were related simply to the cost of finance. The decision to invest and method of finance chosen were likely to be simultaneous in sales-aid leasing where often no alternative is offered. Since most lessors had been involved in other sectors of lending their replies reflected a broader range of experience of investment decision-making than leasing alone.

Information was also sought from lessors on who took the leasing decision within the firm and to whom they referred. Without exception it was thought that the decision to lease was made at a senior level (managing director, finance director, treasurer, senior manager, etc.). Many lessors pointed out that an authorised signature was required on the lease contract and therefore the ultimate sanction lay with the owners or directors of a company. The decision to lease rarely varied because finance decisions were made at the 'top' of organisations – buyers or operations managers might identify a need for a particular asset but unless authorised to do so they did not make decisions on the method of finance chosen. This was also a cause of separation of the two decisions in many firms. While the Board of Directors approved investment proposals, the treasurer or finance director often had considerable latitude in choosing the method of finance.

Clearly small ticket leasing, or at least small ticket relative to the size of the company, is excluded from this high level of authorisation. However, these views tend to run counter to the theory that one of the reasons for the attractiveness of leasing is that it enables more junior managers or those in subsidiaries to get round capital spending constraints. In part, this might be because the people we talked to tended to be involved with the bigger deals. It also might reflect that the lessee would have a natural unwillingness to admitting to circumventing the rules of company policy.

Methods of lease evaluation identified ranged widely from rough rule of thumb methods (comparisons of flat rates, annual percentage rates, etc) to very sophisticated computer packages. Net present value and internal rate of return evaluations were generally considered to be used more by larger companies, whereas smaller companies favoured payback period. Lessors indicated that very often the degree of sophistication on the part of lessees was related to the size of the company, the larger the company the more advanced the lease evaluation method used. However, it was suggested that care must be taken in making such generalisations as there are a number of factors (e.g. the degree of use of leasing) which might affect evaluation practice.

The inadequacies of the means of assessment of investment needs and investment decisions in both private companies and public sector institutions has been frequently noted and brought out recently in the work of the Finance for Industry Committee and the Building and Civil Engineering Little Neddies.

The role and use of external advisers in the decision-making process was also considered by lessors to be related to size of lease company. Small- and medium-sized companies tended to be guided by external advice from accountants, whereas large companies would have specialist internal accountants. One lessor pointed out that companies did not often seek advice on small items of capital equipment. A number of the respondents had clearing banks as parent institutions and said that from time to time clients were introduced by branch bank managers. However, it was generally felt that such bankers still had a limited knowledge of leasing (one company was currently running a course to make managers more aware of leasing), and would use their leasing subsidiaries as a last resort when they were unable or unwilling to lend themselves.

This is in contrast to the approach of some of the overseas banks operating in London whom we interviewed, where a much more comprehensive approach to the financial needs of their customers was followed, as discussed in Section 3.2.

Lease brokers and merchant banks were also mentioned by respondents as external advisers. One lessor pointed out that lessees already using leasing as a method of finance often did not consider other methods or seek external advice when replacing assets that were already leased. It was also indicated that potential lessees generally compared quotations between a number of leasing companies and there was little loyalty to one particular lessor. This therefore reveals one of the classic facts of market penetration. The initial sale requires a major decision and a change in behaviour. Repeat purchases do not require such a major appraisal and hence existing business tends to be consolidated – that is, until the next innovation comes along. However, the lack of customer loyalty is much more interesting. In the first place, it confirms the remarks about the unbundling of financial services which runs rather against the attitude of the clearing banks with respect to retail services. It also helps provide evidence in support of leasing being treated in a different manner from other forms of finance.

We tried to follow this up with lessors but many different opinions were expressed on the question of whether lessors compete directly with other forms of finance. This varied from saying it was a direct competitor with all other forms of finance and purchase, to suggesting that leasing was a unique form of finance. It is interesting to observe that specialist lessors tended to regard leasing as being a unique form of finance, whilst those companies offering a range of facilities took a much wider view of the role of leasing in relation to the use of other forms of finance.

The majority of respondents quoted non-financial factors in the decision-making process which they thought were important. Specific factors mentioned included:

— convenience,
— speed,
— prestige in acquiring new equipment (especially agriculture),
— technological change,
— maintenance and service agreements.

These non-financial advantages related to the ease of concluding the transaction and getting the equipment in place, on the one hand, and the advantages of being able to keep up to date, on the other. Because in many cases the lessor was a much larger company, it found the procedure of purchase much easier than the lessee would have done. Indeed, many lessors of fairly standard equipment were able to reap major advantages from multiple purchases, thus further increasing the cost advantages of leasing if some of this gain was passed on. Similarly, even with finance leasing it could often be easier to keep up to date with the product and upgrade or replace it if it were felt necessary.

It was stressed that whereas in the early 1970s leasing was not regarded as a 'respectable' form of finance, and for this reason many companies which would have benefited from leasing did not use it, it has now become well accepted and fashionable to lease. There has thus been a switch from underutilisation of leasing for non-financial or even prejudicial reasons towards, if anything, the other pole where some companies have leased in situations where other forms of finance might be more suitable.

### 3.1.6    The Quantity and Timing of Investment

The central point of our study is the hypothesis that leasing has led to increased investment and moreover that such investment also has been cyclically affected, being even higher than otherwise in a recession when profitability is low. We therefore faced lessors with these two issues directly and questioned them on whether they considered leasing had affected the quantity and timing of investment. Most lessors felt that leasing had increased the level of investment undertaken by firms but were on the whole unable to quantify the effect. Comments ranged from leasing having a very large impact on the quantity of investments to a suggestion that its effects might only operate at the margin through lowering the cost of capital.

The reasons given for the increase in the quantity of investment brought about by leasing naturally tax advantages (lowering financial costs), cash flow and off-balance sheet aspects. One lessor felt the effect was most apparent in the period 1977 to 1982 when leasing was a relatively cheap source of finance to tax-exhausted firms. However, one of the reasons why the answers were somewhat qualified was that taxable capacity on the part of the lessors was seen as a limiting factor to growth. Nevertheless, these replies did not give us the sort of firm conclusions we would have liked.

The counter-cyclical aspects of leasing we anticipated were also identified, operating through the tax mechanism, but it was thought that even in an upswing some very capital-intensive firms may not make sufficient profit to absorb capital allowances fully, thus weakening the effect. Respondents also indicated that the 1984 Budget would in the short term increase the quantity of investment as lessees would wish to take advantage of capital allowances before they were phased out. The interaction of leasing and Regional Development Grants was also thought to have a stimulative effect on investment, either by being built into the lease agreement as a reduction in rentals, or increasing the value of the grant to non-taxpaying firms. The Regional Development Grant would have been incorporated whatever the form of financing, but leasing companies were also to focus on this and their success in obtaining them.

Comments on the timing effects of leasing ranged from it not being 'particularly marked' to it being 'one of the biggest aspects of leasing'. In general it was felt that leasing had in fact brought forward investment. Regional Development Grants were again mentioned but various other reasons were given for the timing effects of leasing on investment.

While emphasis was put on the tax aspect of leasing including 'year-end' effects and cash flow advantages, not all lessors could quantify the effects. The 'year-end' effect is particularly interesting as it enables companies in effect to bring forward the financial reward from leasing. The sooner the lessor can report, the quicker the investment can be offset against tax. While on the whole this does not require the early payment of tax, it can be used to offset payments which would otherwise have had to be paid by other parts of the group.

The actual time periods cited for bringing forward expenditure ranged widely from one month to one year. The length of bringing forward depended to a large extent on the reason given for affecting timing. However, it was clear that such timing effects as had been perceived were thought to be, on the whole, fairly limited in duration. It was pointed out that a firm may on average wait twenty-three months to obtain capital allowances whereas a lessor may only wait nine months so that an immediate benefit was apparent.

The 1984 Budget was often mentioned by the respondents and one lessor asserted that the timing effects were not important in the past but had become so in the post-Budget period and would continue to be until March 1986. In so far as companies look at the fine details, some may lease during certain periods of the year 'to get their tax position right'. Such considerations apply to both lessors and lessees as each has tax liabilities which could be offset by investments.

### 3.1.7   Trends in Leasing

Although we could only test the validity of our hypotheses by comparing past behaviour against them, much of the usefulness of the analysis is dependent upon estimating what the consequences will be in the future. The future is obviously going to be different from the past because of the 1984 Finance Act, but major differences in outlook depend upon (i) the extent to which full market penetration has been achieved and leasing has become a mature product having reached its long run market share, (ii) likely innovations and new products. To try to tackle both these questions lessors were invited to comment on past and possible future trends in the nature of leasing agreements in respect of size, term, degree of risk taken and the use of variation clauses.

The evidence offered on trends in the size of leases was somewhat contradictory and perhaps reflected the differing market sectors within which the companies interviewed operated, as some remarks were clearly at variance with the known behaviour of the market as a whole. It was also stipulated by a respondent that growth in the size of lease had varied, increasing to 1977, decreasing in the period 1978–81, and in 1982–3 the increase was due to inflation alone – however, most information was non-quantitative. Interestingly, the sales-aid lessor was able to give some figures to illustrate the increase in size. In 1974, the average size of lease was £750 increasing to £1200 in 1979 and to £1500–2000 in 1982 and would continue to increase as assets became more sophisticated. It was felt by some that after March 1986 an increase in size might ensue whilst others projected a movement towards smaller leases. Thus all in all we were not able to form a clear picture.

The term of leasing agreements, according to respondent companies, would seem to have remained fairly stable at five to seven years, although longer leases had become much more common in recent years. The direct link with the life of the asset was stressed and two lessors suggested that they would like to see three-year terms as the useful life of certain assets was tending to become much shorter but this was likely to be unpopular with lessees. Future developments were not clear. Some lessors thought, especially those at the big ticket end of the market, that the term of leases would be increased when only 25 per cent writing down allowances were available; others postulated that there would be little change. However, at that time it appeared to us that convention played the largest role with only a limited role for more sophisticated economic influences.

Lessors emphasised that the creditworthiness of the potential lessee was a key factor in considering the degree of risk to be taken. Although underwriting terms had not changed specifically, companies were perhaps looking more carefully (especially in operating leasing) at proposals in the light of recessionary tendencies in the economy. We obtained the distinct impression that, except for large deals and for marginal companies, the degree of scrutiny was relatively limited.

The use of variation clauses in leasing contracts was discussed.

Although many lessors offered both fixed and variable interest rates, fixed terms were still strongly in demand. This applied especially to small ticket leasing, whereas variable rates were more attractive to large leasing transactions. Taxation variation clauses (corporation tax and capital allowances) had either been used for long periods or introduced quite recently in the last four or five years. Our own rationalisation of the existence of these two groups was that a choice had been made initially but that since neither group had suffered or gained in the early years there had been little incentive to change. However, when lessors experienced adverse movements in tax rates they rapidly changed to prevent a repetition of the experience. The exception was a specialist sales-aid lessor who had never introduced tax variation clauses because this was seen as undesirable in terms of marketing (and indeed had only offered variable interest rates for a ten week period in 1974 as a result of inflationary pressure). Following the 1984 Budget proposals the situation with regard to tax variation clauses had become complex and had caused considerable realignment on the part of some lessors.

Lessors were asked to consider likely future market trends in leasing. The 1984 Budget which removed much of the tax advantage to leasing is clearly expected to change both the nature of leasing and the structure of the industry fundamentally. However, lessors did not indicate that significant changes had already taken place at the time of interview but expected them to become more evident after March 1985 and particularly after March 1986. While this may have all been overtaken by history, we thought it worth pointing out as it indicates that the main protagonists in the industry actually had a rather limited feel for the way it was in practice influenced by tax advantage.

The expected rush of business to take advantage of 75 per cent capital allowances had not been experienced by all lessors interviewed (especially in the South West which is regarded by some as a weak area for leasing business), and comments ranged from describing the present market as being very buoyant to observing that there had been no particular upsurge in new business. However, it was generally felt that current leasing rates were attractive and lessors capacity was high. This, of course, proved to be a major understatement.

Although lessors' opinions of the current state of the market tended to vary somewhat, a broad concensus was apparent on the likely position after March 1986. Clearly the volume of leasing would fall but it was felt that leasing would not vanish and a large portion would remain for non-tax reasons. The main forecast changes were:

(i) *for market sectors*:

— the small ticket sector which is generally not so tax sensitive will be largely unaffected and could possibly expand;

— the medium ticket sector will decline (some said that it will disappear completely) but leasing for non-tax related reasons may remain;

— big ticket leasing will continue where even a 25 per cent writing down allowance can be advantageous.

Thus the picture was for some squeeze at the upper end, high pressure in the middle range, but little effect on the smaller end, but no sensible magnitudes could be attached to these changes.

(ii) *for the Nature of Leasing*:

— finance leasing will fall away sharply in favour of operating leasing where residual values are of importance (some lessors indicated that residual values might pose a problem since they did not currently possess the relevant specialist knowledge required – one lessor suggested more use would be made of residual value insurance and bank guarantees; another thought that large lessors may acquire existing companies with such expertise);

— 'non-recourse' leverage leasing used in the USA could be introduced into the UK if approved by the Inland Revenue. There are basically three parties involved in such a lease structure – the lessor, the lessee and a provider of long-term debt. In essence this form of leasing works in the following manner. The lessor funds only a proportion of the purchase price of an asset and borrows the remainder from a financial institution. In some cases there may in fact be more than one lessor or lender involved in the transaction. The lessor leases the asset to the lessee but, as security for the loan, the rentals are assigned to the lender who also holds a mortgage over the asset. In the event of default by the lessee the lender has no recourse to the lessor whose risk is therefore limited only to the extent of his investment in the asset. Nevertheless, the lessor can still benefit fully from any tax advantage associated with the transaction. As a result of these factors lessors are able to offer reduced rentals to lessees. Such leases have been common in the USA but difficulty has been experienced in introducing them into the UK because of problems in assessing the tax implications. These principally revolve around the question of whether interest paid by the lessor on the loan element is deductible for tax purposes.

Other areas of difficulty involve the situation where the loan is made to a subsidiary company which can affect the overall tax position of the parent group of companies, and the question of whether capital expenditure is incurred at the outset or when the loan is repayable (if the latter is the case then the benefit of any capital allowances will be delayed and the transaction will be rendered less attractive).

— A switch may occur from leasing to a form of industrial hire purchase, but there will still be a demand for medium-term asset based finance.

(iii) *Structural Changes*:

— Overall there will be a fall in the number of lessors. This will apply particularly to non-financial lessors as the tax advantage diminishes and margins are not so attractive. Having said this, sales-aid leasing will remain where manufacturers have existing arrangements and it is suggested that this type of leasing could expand similar to existing practice in the USA.

— Lessors will move into other areas of medium-term finance reflecting a move to hire purchase indicated above – one lessor already is not marketing leasing aggressively and is encouraging its staff to obtain hire purchase business.

— Lease-brokers will decline in accordance with the changes expected in the market.

— Foreign banks will move into the market when the tax advantage is no longer with domestic institutions.

It is interesting to note that one lessor suggested that the leasing market would have seen some decline irrespective of the tax changes announced in the 1984 Budget, because as the position of the economy

improves the demand for leasing would decline in favour of traditional bank borrowing as bankers become more confident and are
willing to lend to industry.

## 3.2  THE MAJOR LESSOR SURVEY

Interviews with major lessors were conducted during April and May
1985. The actual structure of the interviews was intentionally somewhat less rigid than the South West Survey with the object of
encouraging a broad discussion of the historical and future nature of
leasing in the UK. Care was taken to avoid any bias that might
possibly have arisen by 'leading' the respondents with specific information gained in the South West Survey although, of course, the
basic format of the structured interview was developed from the
previous study.

The interview began with an introduction by the interviewer cov-
ering an outline of the research project aims and objectives. Respondents were then asked to quantify their comments where necessary in
the discussion that was to follow by reference to particular types of
leasing (i.e. finance or operating) and market sectors (i.e. small,
medium and big ticket leasing).

A relatively small sample of the six major lessors was drawn (all
members of the Equipment Leasing Association), but in terms of
rental income for the year 1984 these companies represented approximately 65 per cent of rents received by Equipment Leasing
Association members. The majority of business transacted by these
companies is finance leasing and ranged across the market from small
ticket leasing to sizeable large ticket transactions.

Because of the size of sample and the nature of the interviews, no
statistical inference can be drawn but it is helpful to summarise the
various points that arose and their relation to the survey in the South
West.

### 3.2.1  Are Some Assets, Firms or Circumstances Particularly Suited to Leasing?

Like the South West Survey, much of the interview concentrated on
the manner in which lessors considered leasing had affected the
investment behaviour of firms. Lessors were asked initially to identify
apparent correlations between the use of leasing and factors such as

the size of lessee firm, organisational/legal structure, industry, sector, etc. In general, respondents felt that no strong relationship exists between leasing and such characteristics. Indeed, lessors indicated that leasing was used in all industries and sectors by all types of firms and there was really no identifiable 'typical' lessee. However, certain areas of interest were mentioned. It was suggested by one respondent that subsidiaries of both foreign and domestic companies were particularly drawn to leasing for budgetary reasons such as avoiding capital expenditure limits. It was also pointed out in this section that in the early development of leasing in the UK, leasing initially had a 'poor image' as a method of funding and that there was little activity at the 'small end' of the market. It was not until around 1976 that leasing became a 'respectable' source of finance. This followed the findings of the South West Survey closely. A further interesting comment was made relating to movement in the market; one firm which had used leasing, subsequently for tax shelter reasons, assumed the role of corporate lessor but then later reverted to being a lessee, only its taxation position shifted again.

Respondents were then invited to comment on the circumstances in which leasing is used. Discussion ranged widely and it would seem that there exists a broad spectrum of situations in which leasing might be considered appropriate. Specific areas identified included:

— The ability of medium-sized companies to increase gearing through off-balance sheet finance.

— Tax advantage.

— Major projects which take time to 'come on stream'.

— Fast growing companies which need to maximise funding options (this was also linked to the fact that such companies may not show a substantial profit and therefore have very little tax shelter).

— Well-established companies in temporary difficulties, particularly in a recessionary period, where leasing was essentially counter-cyclical in nature (it was estimated by one lessor that given the tax structure before March 1984, leasing provided a cheap source of funds at approximately half the cost of traditional bank borrowing).

These remarks therefore identified a series of market niches which leasing could fill, several of which were not primarily tax related.

In addition to identifying situations in which leasing had been used, it was also observed that in the past (1975–83) lessors tended to take a longer view of funding than the banks and provided seven to ten year fixed finance which at the time was difficult to obtain from banks. In the context of the financing of British industry, this lack of medium- to long-term finance has been cited by many as an important con- tributory factor to the relative failure of British manufacturing industry to invest, innovate and maintain long-term international competitive- ness (see House of Lords, 1985). In that House of Lords Report, on Overseas Trade, this comparison is made most clearly with respect to Japan and West Germany.

This feature of the gains from leasing will be more than can appear from a study of mere numerical values, as it could lead to more than proportionately valuable investment (in terms of long run rate of return) and meet a need where there was no other ready substitute.

Data were again sought on the type of investment goods that have been leased. Here respondents were required not only to identify market trends over the past decade in types of asset leased, but also trends in the size and length of leases; whether in fact there was any evidence to suggest that leasing had, as a method of funding, pro- moted technological change; and finally whether there were specific assets which tend only to be financed by leasing. It was generally indicated that all types of asset have been leased in the past decade. Initially, the market had concentrated on vehicles (including con- tainers) but subsequently leasing developed to become used exten- sively for all types of asset, particularly plant and machinery. In recent years, the market had experienced growth in the leasing of large plant and machinery (e.g. that used by the oil industry). This really takes leasing beyond the traditional image of movable, resale- able, identifiable assets. However, while it has in fact been possible to move an oil refinery some of these large assets are most specific both to their use and the place of use.

Leases, especially at the large ticket end of the market, had tended to increase in size and term, although in the small to medium range five to seven years was still the norm. It was stressed by most lessors that they tended to look to the creditworthiness of a client as being the most important factor in a leasing transaction, rather than the particular type of asset which, although important, tended to play somewhat of a secondary role, echoing what was said in the South West Survey. Finance leasing was not thought to encourage techno- logical change as penalty clauses often exist which discourage the rapid replacement of assets before the end of an agreement. However, one lessor pointed out that specialist operating leasing companies dealing in assets such as computers may see a much closer relationship. Even so, there may be an incentive to promote technological change if lessors tend to deal in the most up to date equipment in order to maximise their second-hand value, or if leasing leads to a shorter asset life with people replacing quickly after the expiry of the primary lease period. It is not quite clear why they should do that, except under pressure from lessors hoping for a new primary period on a replacement asset, as secondary period rentals are likely to be relatively small.

Certain assets such as reprographic equipment and computers are areas where leasing finance tends to be dominant. This does not, of course, imply by itself that leasing helped increase investment in this area. It also reported that special projects such as oil refineries had attracted lease financing and had drawn foreign investment to the UK. This would be a clear example of a difference at the margin in attracting investment from foreign multinationals – or indeed in discouraging UK firms from investing overseas. That question of the desirability of such direct investment – in either direction – has been the subject of considerable controversy, much of it on non-economic grounds. This is not the place to debate the issue, merely to note that a series of factors affect the siting of major investments of this form, of which leasing is one. The others include regional grants, local tax holdings, guarantees of the ability to repatriate profits, pollution restrictions, protection of market share from further entrants and many others. It is almost impossible to say which one was the deciding factor as they cannot be ordered in any meaningful manner.

### 3.2.2 Why Is Leasing Used by Firms?

Discussion concerning the reasons leasing is used by firms was divided into the following factors:

#### (i) Tax-based Leasing

The role of tax-based leasing was discussed first in terms of its importance in the development of leasing in the UK, and secondly in relation to the fiscal changes introduced in the 1984 Budget and the position after March 1986, when the reforms of corporate tax will have been fully implemented.

Without exception, it was indicated that tax-based leasing had played an important role in the growth of UK leasing, with one lessor suggesting that until 1984 all leasing from the perspective of his company had been tax-based with another estimating a figure of 90 per cent of leasing.

In the transitional period to March 1986, it was forecast that the volume of leasing would increase substantially (although initially the market had been slow to react), but would subsequently show a sharp decline (estimated by one lessor to be a fall of 50 per cent of the 1984 volume of business given at some £4 billion by the Equipment Leasing Association) as leasing rates become comparatively less competitive. It was also suggested that major lessees are likely to leave the market if they are not still attracted to leasing by other factors such as fixed rentals or off-balance sheet finance.

### (ii)   Cash Flow

Lessors considered cash flow advantages to be an important reason to lease. Some respondents stressed budgetary advantages in identifying and matching costs to revenue (in the case of groups of companies leasing enabled the cost of an asset to be accurately charged to a member company), and one lessor felt this would increase in importance as a reason to lease when most of the tax advantage had been removed after March 1986. However, it was pointed out that the banks are now much more flexible in terms of loans (e.g. granting 'capital holidays') and therefore this might not hold. It was also indicated that leasing had been used historically to circumvent central bank credit controls on other forms of funding.

### (iii)   Additional Source of Finance

Lessors were asked to comment on the effects of leasing on the debt capacity of firms within the following framework of alternatives:

— Does leasing replace debt on a pound for pound basis and, if so, why?

— Does leasing lead to more finance being available and, if so, why? (Here it was intended that the off-balance sheet nature of leasing and the possible effects of SSAP 21 should be discussed. Other topics for discussion were to include the question of whether lessors took a larger risk than 'traditional' lenders and the role of residual value.)

— Does leasing displace debt on a more than pound for pound basis and, if so, why?

Respondents found this a difficult section and in fact some lessors preferred to refrain from answering. However, a number were willing to respond, although often in a limited manner. It was thought by some that firms do equate leasing and borrowing with a framework of preferred debt to equity ratio. Equally, others held that leasing could on occasion increase the gearing of a company through off-balance sheet effects. Opinion seemed to be divided on the question of the importance of off-balance sheet finance, with some lessors suggesting that bankers often did not take leasing into account whilst others felt that banks had been aware of it since its early development. It was generally thought that the effect of the implementation of SSAP 21 would be to encourage movement both by lessors and lessees towards operating-type leasing contracts. There was little evidence that leasing had displaced debt on a more than pound for pound basis. On the question of risk-taking and residual value, lessors suggested that the underwriting of leases was at least, if not more, stringent than the underwriting of other forms of finance and, in terms of finance leasing, residual value was not of significance. It was suggested that this may be relevant for smaller higher risk-bearing leasing companies where the asset was used more as security.

Some of these remarks strike right at the heart of our analysis. If there is only one for one displacement of debt by leasing, then leasing can be little more than a contribution to profitability at the Government's expense (through a lower yield on corporate taxes).

### (iv) Others

Under this heading, other 'traditional' advantages of leasing (i.e. fixed contract, flexibility, etc) were discussed and it was generally felt that although in the past these had tended to be important in specific instances, their overall importance would now increase with the removal of widespread tax advantages after March 1986.

### 3.2.3 Leasing and the Quantity and Timing of Investment

In the section of the interview that followed, respondents were asked to consider the effects of leasing on the quantity and timing of investment in three distinct time periods – (i) over the past decade up to 1984, (ii) the position in the period 1984–6, and (iii) post March 1986. They were asked to relate their remarks to the reasons for leasing, which they had discussed previously, and to lessors' tax capacity.

Most lessors asserted that leasing had in fact increased the level of investment over the past decade through tax advantage, but were unable to quantify the effect. Instead, examples of large projects were given where it was considered that without leasing, investment would not have occurred. One such example was the financing of a catalytic cracking plant at Milford Haven in Wales, which, it was thought, without leasing and the benefit of Regional Development Grants, would certainly have been located in France. A further example was the siting of the Nissan car plant in the UK. In addition to these relatively large projects, shipping was given as an instance where without leasing much would have been built abroad. Against the view that leasing had increased investment, one lessor suggested that if an investment is sound it would take place irrespective of tax advantage. However, this view must take the word 'sound' to mean 'having a larger expected rate of return'. This does not negate the possible advantage of leasing at the margin or the ability to undertake a wider range of projects for the same outlay.

The majority of lessors agreed that leasing has also affected the timing of investment, but felt that the time period involved was not particularly long – certainly it was thought by many to be less than a year. One lessor felt that it had perhaps brought forward investment in 1979 which otherwise would have been delayed. This therefore agrees with the views in the South West: that the likely affect is positive but of unquantifiable size; that timing may have been effected, but only to a limited extent and for a fairly short period of time.

The position regarding the transitional period to March 1986 was unclear. Respondents felt that the surge in leasing was obviously tax led, but it was difficult to distinguish between this and a general increase in overall investment.

After March 1986 the level of investment through leasing would fall away sharply, being determined by the degree to which leasing was previously tax based. Lessors here again referred to the estimates given in the previous section on lessee behaviour. One lessor made the point that car leasing had historically survived the withdrawal of 100 per cent allowances and perhaps this pattern would be reflected in the future market. Here one has to consider whether there are other aspects of vehicle leasing which have sustained it – particularly in regard to what is often largely an operating leasing environment – before deciding whether the analogy applies to leasing as a whole after 1986.

The next section of the interview comprised a discussion of the nature and significance of the various suppliers of lease finance in the leasing market prior to the 1984 Budget. It also sought evidence of change since then and likely future developments both in terms of market structure and leasing agreements.

Lessors commented that originally the leasing market had consisted principally of financial institutions. It was noted that there had been occasions when tax capacity had been in short supply and some lessors had temporarily left the market in such circumstances. The late 1970s saw the entry of corporate non-financial lessors into the market and respondents felt that this had undoubtedly increased competition and forced leasing rates down. Foreign-owned lessors had been active in the market but not to any significant extent. Sales-aid leasing had expanded since the mid 1970s.

After March 1986 it was thought that the following changes were likely to occur:

— Corporate lessors will leave the market (a number have already reputedly 'sold their books') and leasing will revert to the financial sector.

— Sales-aid leasing (which has been historically less tax sensitive) will expand as evidenced by the considerable interest shown by the industry in this type of leasing.

— Foreign banks will enter the market as the tax advantage to domestic leasing companies declines.

— Merchant banks are likely to concentrate on advising clients and 'packaging' finance.

— The volume of leasing business transacted in the leasing market will undoubtedly decline and future expansion will depend on lessors' ability to adapt to the new tax regime.

— In the past, demand has been such that there has been little pressure to innovate. Lessors have a mix of skills in taxation and fixed asset finance. These skills will still be needed after March 1986 and will be used to develop new products, particularly in the areas of project finance and leveraged leasing.

— Leasing rates by March 1986 will tend to move into line with other borrowing rates and pressure is likely to occur in the middle market which in the past has been notably 'rate sensitive'.

— Even more importance will be laid upon residual value and there will be a general movement towards operating leasing (this may be re-enforced by the implications of SSAP 21), but at this stage it is questionable whether the major financial lessors have the required expertise in equipment values.

By the time this book is published and read it will be possible to form a view on the validity of these forecasts on the basis of revealed experience. Initial indications are that lessors were unduly pessimistic.

## 3.3   IMPLICATIONS

In relation to the central hypotheses, both the 'South West Survey' and the 'Major Lessor Survey' have clearly indicated that the majority of interviewees considered that leasing had in fact increased the level of investment and that tax advantage has played an important role in this process. Although lessors were unable to quantify the effect of leasing on investment, some particularly significant examples of major projects were given where leasing had been largely influential in the investment decision. However, it is interesting to note that some lessors felt that leasing may have only affected investment at the margin, a point to which we shall return later and furthermore that if an investment project is viable then it will proceed irrespective of tax implications. In addition, the survey has shown that non-tax advantages have also been instrumental in the decision to lease and the relationship between leasing and investment. It has also been demonstrated that lessors generally perceive that, largely as a consequence of tax based factors, leasing has changed the time profile of investment, although there would appear to be no general consensus of the precise mechanism and magnitude of this effect. Considerable further evidence is thus required before we can draw any clear conclusions.

# 4 The Use of Leasing by Firms

## 4.1 BACKGROUND

The structured interviews conducted with lessors provided considerable insight into leasing activity in the UK and into the role of leasing in relation to investment behaviour. The results suggest that the use of leasing has led to both a higher level of investment expenditure and to favourable retiming of it (by bringing it forward in times of recession) largely through tax incentives, although other important determinants were also identified. While the evidence gathered from lessors has delineated possible effects of leasing on firms' investment decisions, it is primarily useful as a guide to obtaining further conclusive information since it provides largely subjective data which are dependent upon the interviewees' perception of factors that affect investment through leasing. Clearly, it is not reasonable simply to assume that the factors considered by lessors to be significant in the investment process will necessarily coincide with those perceived by lessees. Consequently, in order to extend the basic background analysis, a postal questionnaire survey of leasing behaviour was undertaken with the express intention of obtaining data from actual decision-makers in individual firms.

Although there is an immediate attraction in taking this direct approach, in practice there are several difficulties involved in the application of survey techniques to the study of investment.[1] Firms' investment decisions do not take place in isolation but result from a complex interaction of internal and external determinants which will tend to vary according to the type of asset, the industry of the investing firm and are unlikely to be constant through time.

Investment is a dynamic process and however carefully the questionnaire is constructed it is perhaps questionable whether respondents will be able to identify separate formative influences upon the decision to invest clearly or indeed to estimate their impact reliably. Eisner (1957, p. 514) puts this strongly – 'it is quite possible that the individual businessman does not really know, in any sense satisfactory to the economist, what determines his investment decisions'. The problem is essentially that of distinguishing adequately between the perceptions of respondents in relation to the decision-making process and their actions in reality, which might suggest radically different behavioural patterns from those derived from questionnaire analysis alone. This problem is not unique to investment but applies to many areas of microeconomic decision-making. Individually people may be unaware that they follow various forms of economic reasoning, yet actual observation indicates clearly that they do. The reverse is also true, people may argue that they take particular factors into account, yet their actual behaviour is inconsistent with doing so.

Furthermore, respondents' perceptions may often be specific to the particular firm and factors which appear to be significant at this level may not be so in aggregate, either because of the uniqueness of the individual case which becomes unimportant when many results are added together or because other individuals have contrary motivations which cancel out upon addition.

Nevertheless, whilst fully accepting that there are definite limitations to the technique, the questionnaire survey was undertaken to examine the leasing behaviour of firms because satisfactory data does not exist at present either for individual firms or in aggregate.

Earlier studies of the leasing behaviour of firms in the UK have not sought to investigate the impact of leasing on investment *per se* but have tended either to be examinations of specific areas or to have formed part of more generalised work on leasing. Fawthrop and Terry (1975) examined debt management and the use of leasing based on a questionnaire survey of senior financial executives of fifty-four major corporations which was followed up by interviews. Sykes (1976), in a study of the lease–buy decision aimed at introducing companies to leasing and understanding the advantages and disadvantages of alternative methods of finance, included a postal questionnaire survey of leasing practice in 202 member companies of the British Institute of Management. Tomkins, Lowe and Morgan (1979) in their analysis of the financial leasing industry considered the significance of leasing to small firms. Some questions on leasing were inserted into interviews with eighty-four companies which formed part of a larger project on the financial profile of small rapidly growing firms up to the stage of flotation. Hull and Hubbard (1980) carried out a survey of the leasing industry by questionnaire/ interviews to investigate the mode of operations, attitudes and decision of criteria of lessors, lessee and leasebrokers. However, although these studies were not primarily concerned with the question of whether leasing had affected investment, it is of relevance to the present study that each of them included an examination of the reasons for leasing and, in particular, assessment of the importance of tax advantage. The results of their research are discussed later in the analysis of the questionnaire replies.


## 4.2 THE NATURE OF THE SURVEY

The broad aims of the survey were to investigate the past behaviour of firms with respect to leasing and the effects of leasing on the level and timing of investment. This investigation included an examination of the extent, methods and effects of sales-aid, leasing which may also influence investment. In addition, the survey sought to assess the general impact of the 1984 Budget on the use of leasing.

The specific objectives of the questionnaire were to obtain data on the following:

1. types of leasing used;
2. types of asset leased;
3. firms' policies towards leasing;
4. factors taken into account by firms when deciding to lease;
5. factors taken into account by firms when deciding not to lease;
6. effects of leasing on the quantity and timing of investment;
7. extent and method of sales-aid leasing;
8. effects of sales-aid leasing on the quantity and timing of sales;
9. amount of leasing undertaken since the 1984 Budget;
10. the use of leasing after March 1986.

The survey was conducted in September 1985 using two samples – a sample of mainly small to medium companies in the South West Economic Planning Region (Avon, Cornwall, Devon, Dorset, Gloucestershire, Somerset and Wiltshire) drawn from *Kompass*; and a sample of companies generally of above average size formed by the National Institute of Economic and Social Research (NIESR) representing a range of commerce and industry. The rationale of using two samples was to allow for possible differences in behaviour as a result of generalised size factors.

### 4.2.1  The Survey of the South West

Questionnaires were sent to 1000 companies in the South West Economic Plannning Region and replies were received from 406 companies which, after making necessary adjustments to the sample for companies that replied as a group rather than individual units (5) and for companies no longer at the address to which the question-naire was sent (27), represents a response rate of 41.9 per cent. Companies in both samples were classified by size and by industry. The number of employees for each company was used as an indicator of size and companies were grouped by industry according to the Standard Industrial Classification (1980) broad divisions. The distri-bution of companies surveyed in the South West by size and by industry is shown in Tables 4.1 and 4.2 respectively.
This distribution of the 406 companies responding to the question-naire by size and by industry are also shown in Tables 4.1 and 4.2.

Although the proportions responding vary across the categories, there are no glaring discrepancies and any problems of bias due to non-response are therefore likely to be common to all categories.

A response of over 40 per cent to a survey sent out to a random sample like this is extremely good and we are very grateful to all those who took the time and effort to reply. Perhaps it is a reflection of the importance which they attach to leasing.

*Table* 4.1   Distribution of companies surveyed by size (South West Econ-omic Planning Region)

|  | Companies surveyed[1] | | Companies responding number (%) |
|---|---|---|---|
| Size (number of employees) | Number of companies | Percentage of total | |
| up to 100 | 600 (575) | 60.0 (59.5) | 191   (47.0) |
| 101 to 500 | 300 (293) | 30.0 (30.2) | 131   (32.3) |
| 501 to 1000 | 50 | 5.0  (5.2) | 23   (5.7) |
| more than 1000 | 50[2] | 5.0  (5.2) | 23[4]   (5.7) |
| unidentified[3] | – | – | 38   (9.3) |
| Total | 1000 (968) | 100.0 | 406 (100.0) |

[1] Adjustments to the original sample are shown in brackets.
[2] Includes 29 companies with over 2000 employees.
[3] Questionnaires returned without company identity.
[4] Includes 14 companies with over 2000 employees.

*Table* 4.2  Distribution of companies surveyed by industry (South West Economic Planning Region)

| Industry group | | Companies surveyed[1] | | Companies responding number (%) |
|---|---|---|---|---|
| | | Number of companies | Percentage of total | |
| 0 | Agriculture, forestry and fishing | 0 | 0.0 | 0 (0.0) |
| 1 | Energy and water supply industries | 6 | 0.6 | 4 (1.0) |
| 2 | Extraction of minerals and ores other than fuels; manufacture of metals, mineral products and chemicals | 63 (59) | 6.3 (6.1) | 24 (5.9) |
| 3 | Metal goods, engineering and vehicle industries | 488 (472) | 48.8 (48.8) | 173 (42.6) |
| 4 | Other manufacturing industries | 288 (278) | 28.8 (28.7) | 112 (27.6) |
| 5 | Construction | 30 | 3.0 (3.1) | 16 (3.9) |
| 6 | Distribution, hotels and catering; repairs | 47 (46) | 4.7 | 16 (3.9) |
| 7 | Transport and communications | 38 (37) | 3.8 | 11 (2.7) |
| 8 | Banking, finance, insurance, business services and leasing | 24 | 2.4 (2.5) | 8 (2.0) |
| 9 | Other services | 16 | 1.6 (1.7) | 4 (1.0) |
| | Unidentified[2] | – | – | 38 (9.4) |
| Total | | 1000 (968) | 100.0 | 406 (100.0) |

[1] Adjustments to the original sample are shown in brackets.
[2] Questionnaires returned without company identity.

### 4.2.2  The NIESR Panel

Questionnaires were also sent to eighty-five companies on the National Institute of Economic and Social Research survey panel and replies were received from thirty companies giving a response rate of 35.3 per cent, a little lower than that in the South West survey which is surprising as the NIESR sample had previously expressed a willingness to answer such questions. The distribution of companies in the total sample by size and by industry are shown in Tables 4.3 and 4.4 respectively as is the distribution of the companies replying.

*Table* 4.3   Distribution of companies surveyed by size (NIESR survey panel of companies)

| | Companies surveyed | | Companies responding (number (%)) |
|---|---|---|---|
| Size (number of employees) | Number of companies | Percentage of total | |
| up to 10 000 | 37[1] | 43.5 | 12[2]  (40.0) |
| 10 001 to 50 000 | 30 | 35.3 | 9   (30.0) |
| 50 001 to 100 000 | 11 | 13.0 | 6   (20.0) |
| more than 100 000 | 7 | 8.2 | 3   (10.0) |
| Total | 85 | 100.0 | 30  (100.0) |

[1] Includes 20 companies with over 2000 employees.
[2] Includes 7 companies with over 2000 employees.

Here response rates are sufficiently low that the validity of the response must be questioned for several of the smaller categories. The complete absence of companies in categories 7, 8 and 9; Transport, Communications, Banking, Finance, etc, Services, and Other services is also a matter for regret.

## 4.3   THE RESULTS

The questionnaire was divided into three sections – (A) 'Use of leasing to finance capital investment'; (B) 'Non-use of leasing to finance capital investment'; and (C) 'Leasing as a marketing device'. Of the 406 companies replying to the questionnaire in the South West Economic Planning Region, 268 (66 per cent) had in fact used leasing and 138 (34 per cent) had not, whilst of the 30 respondent companies from the NIESR survey panel 26 (86.7 per cent) had used leasing and only 4 (13.3 per cent) had not.

In Section A, 'Use of leasing to finance capital investment', there were four initial questions included concerning (i) company policy towards leasing, (ii) forms of leasing used, (iii) types of asset leased, and (iv) factors taken into account in the decision to lease. These were each divided into two distinct time periods – the past financial year and five years ago. This division was intended to distinguish changes in behavioural patterns over time, particularly in respect of the effects of the Finance Act 1984. The results of the questionnaire are presented in the discussion that follows which does not necess-

*Table* 4.4   Distribution of companies surveyed by industry (NIESR survey panel of companies)

| | Companies surveyed | | Companies responding (number (%)) |
|---|---|---|---|
| Industry group | Number of companies | Percentage of total | |
| 0  Agriculture, forestry and fishing | 0 | 0.00 | 0   (0.0) |
| 1  Energy and water supply industries | 5 | 5.9 | 2   (6.7) |
| 2  Extraction of minerals and ores other than fuels; manufacture of metals, mineral products and chemicals | 16 | 18.8 | 7  (23.3) |
| 3  Metal goods, engineering and vehicle industries | 28 | 33.0 | 10  (33.3) |
| 4  Other manufacturing industries | 24 | 28.2 | 7  (23.3) |
| 5  Construction | 3 | 3.5 | 2   (6.7) |
| 6  Distribution, hotels and catering; repairs | 9 | 10.6 | 2   (6.7) |
| 7  Transport and communications | 38 (37) | 3.8 | 11   (2.7) |
| 8  Banking, finance, insurance, business services and leasing | 0 | 0 | 0  (0.00) |
| 9  Other services | 0 | 0 | 0  (0.00) |
| Total | 85 | 100.0 | 30 (100.0) |

arily follow the order of questions in the survey, but rather the logical flow of the objectives and underlying hypotheses examined.

In the South West Survey, 223 companies had leased assets in the past financial year and 211 did so five years ago, whilst in the NIESR survey 23 had leased in the past financial year and 25 five year ago. (A breakdown of these figures into the types of leasing used by companies is shown in Tables 4.5 and 4.6.) There is clearly a tendency for the generally larger companies from the NIESR survey panel to use a combination of both finance and operating leasing more extensively in both time periods, although it is the use of finance leasing only which is the most obvious distinguishing feature. In the South West survey of mainly small- to medium-sized compa-

*Table* 4.5   Type of leasing used (number (percentage) of companies)

|  | SOUTH WEST ECONOMIC PLANNING REGION | | NIESR PANEL | |
|---|---|---|---|---|
|  | *Past financial year* | *Five years ago* | *Past financial year* | *Five years ago* |
| Finance leasing only | 112  (50.2) | 120  (56.9) | 9  (39.1) | 10  (40.0) |
| Operating leasing only | 31  (13.9) | 25  (11.9) | 1  (4.4) | 3  (12.0) |
| Both | 78  (35.0) | 64  (30.3) | 13  (56.5) | 12  (48.0) |
| Not specified | 2  (0.9) | 2  (0.9) |  |  |
| Total | 223 (100.0) | 211 (100.0) | 30 (100.0) | 30 (100.0) |

nies the use of finance leasing only has been predominant. However, quite a large proportion of respondent companies have used both types. In each sample the number of companies using operating leasing only has been relatively small. Although there is no indication of the relative proportions of finance leasing and operating leasing in the category 'both', it might reasonably be expected that finance leasing has formed the main element in view of the aggregate statistics. We have argued that the effect on investment behaviour through the tax implications of leasing is likely to be greater in relation to finance leasing than operating leasing. Since operating leasing tends to apply to a more limited range of activities, the probable reason for its wider use by the larger companies is simply that they, by virtue of their size, are likely to cover one of those activities.

A further point of interest arises from the data relating to respondent lessee companies in the South West survey. Although a strict comparison cannot be made, it is interesting to consider the findings of Tomkins, Lowe and Morgan (1979) concerning the types of leasing used by small companies. In their examination of the significance of leasing to small companies, they found that, of eighty-four companies interviewed, seventeen (20 per cent) had used some form of leasing and of these only two had used finance leasing. Whilst acknowledging the difficulties of analysing small numbers, the authors concluded that 'this seems to add weight to our feeling that not much financial leasing was done by small companies at least before 1976'.[2] On the basis of what can be no more than a casual observation as a result of sampling differences, it would appear that the position has changed since then. The survey of companies in the South West sample showed that of companies using finance leasing only in the past financial year, almost 80 per cent had 500 or fewer employees – the equivalent figure for five years ago was marginally over 78 per cent. Of those using both forms of leasing approximately 71 per cent of companies had 500 or fewer employees in both periods. It would seem likely that the use of finance leasing has spread over the last decade.

### 4.3.2 Assets Leased

The lessor survey indicated that a wide range of assets is leased by companies. Table 4.6 shows the number of respondent lessee companies that have leased the various categories of asset included in the questionnaire. In the South West survey the leasing of vehicles is predominant in both time periods. However, there are intertemporal differences in the ranking order of other assets. Five years ago vehicles were followed, in order of the number of companies leasing each type of asset, by office equipment, plant and machinery, and computers. Whereas, in the past financial year, the order had changed to vehicles, computers, office equipment and plant and machinery. This apparent movement towards the increasing importance of computer leasing is particularly relevant in respect of the relationship between technological changes in capital goods and their financing.

It can be argued that leasing has encouraged investment in high technology assets such as computers because of a shift in the risk involved away from the user company. In contrast to the South West

*Table* 4.6   Type of asset leased (number of companies)

| | SOUTH WEST ECONOMIC PLANNING REGION | | NIESR PANEL | |
| | *Past financial year* | *Five years ago* | *Past financial year* | *Five years ago* |
|---|---|---|---|---|
| Plant and machinery | 105 | 95 | 19 | 20 |
| Vehicles | 140 | 117 | 11 | 13 |
| Computers | 117 | 88 | 19 | 20 |
| Office equipment | 108 | 101 | 7 | 5 |
| Other | 10 | 4 | 3 | 3 |

survey, the ranking order has not changed over the two time periods for respondent lessee companies from the NIESR survey panel. Both in the past financial year and five years ago the leasing of plant and machinery and computers has been most prevalent. This is a clear structural difference from the smaller companies.

### 4.3.3 Leasing and Corporate Financial Strategy

*A priori*, the influence of leasing on investment is likely to be greater if its use forms part of a definite corporate financial strategy. The reasons why this might be the case relate to the cost and availability of finance. Firms which are tax exhausted and therefore unable to take immediate advantage of capital allowances may reduce their cost of finance by pursuing a coherent policy of leasing within the overall financing structure. Although previous studies have not tended to demonstrate conclusively that interest rates have a strong influence on investment behaviour, the results from our study suggest that firms will tend to invest more if the cost of finance is reduced. If the systematic use of leasing assists in minimising the cost of finance, then the effect on investment is likely to be more marked when employed as an integral part of the total financing strategy of the firm. In addition to the cost factor, investment will also be determined by the availability of funds.

In periods when internal funds have been limited, and the use of equity finance which avoided the utilisation of debt has become more common, the careful management of leasing within the financial policy may increase the level of debt available to the firm, thereby facilitating investment.

It is worthwhile mentioning here the concept of 'linkage-leasing' put forward by Fawthrop and Terry (1976). It was argued that by using instalment debt cash inflows could be immediately generated for financing other capital expenditures rather than waiting for sufficient inflows to build up for a lump sum expenditure. Through leasing the firm is able to acquire an asset and invest in other assets. Leasing can therefore influence the number of projects undertaken. This is not to argue that leasing may not affect investment if it is used unsystematically, but rather that its impact will be greater if it forms part of a set strategy.

The survey shows that most respondents in both samples at least thought that they had used leasing as part of a corporate financial strategy, although, of course, we do not know precisely what form

*Table* 4.7   Company policy towards leasing (number of companies)

| | SOUTH WEST ECONOMIC PLANNING REGION | | NIESR PANEL | |
|---|---|---|---|---|
| | *Past financial year* | *Five years ago* | *Past financial year* | *Five years ago* |
| As part of a corporate financial strategy | 130 | 101 | 19 | 18 |
| Because no alternative was offered by the supplier | 10 | 10 | 0 | 0 |
| On an *ad hoc* basis | 87 | 98 | 3 | 6 |
| Other | 6 | 5 | 2 | 2 |

this strategy took and the role of leasing within it. The results of the survey in relation to the policy towards the use of leasing is shown in Table 4.7. It is noticeable that leasing on an *ad hoc* basis has also been fairly extensive in the South West survey, particularly in the period five years ago when there was only a marginal difference compared with the number of companies leasing as part of a corporate financial strategy. Captive leasing (i.e. where no alternative was offered by the supplier) does not appear to be very commonplace. Other factors mentioned in relation to the use of leasing in the South West survey included 'equipment for one large contract' and the use of leasing as an experiment; in the NIESR survey 'tooling' and 'for commercial/operating considerations' were put forward as additional reasons.

### 4.3.4   Factors Taken into Account When Deciding to Lease

The survey indicated some behavioural differences in the two samples in relation to factors taken into account when deciding to lease. The central hypothesis of this study suggests that tax advantage should be important in the leasing decision. Table 4.8 shows that in the South West survey (of generally smaller companies) avoiding large capital outlay appears to be the most significant factor, although tax advantage is also clearly important, whereas in the NIESR survey (of, in the main, larger companies) tax advantage is more obviously predominant. A discrepancy of this size suggests that at the smaller end of the market there are some quite different behavioural patterns

*Table* 4.8   Factors taken into account when deciding to lease (number of companies)

| | SOUTH WEST ECONOMIC PLANNING REGION | | NIESR PANEL | |
| | *Past financial year* | *Five years ago* | *Past financial year* | *Five years ago* |
| --- | --- | --- | --- | --- |
| Avoiding large capital outlay | 148 | 145 | 3 | 5 |
| Expanding debt capacity | 31 | 19 | 4 | 4 |
| Tax advantages | 77 | 74 | 18 | 19 |
| Safeguarding against obsolescence | 51 | 35 | 7 | 8 |
| Other | 26 | 19 | 4 | 3 |

from that which apply at the larger end, which is the better documented and more frequently referred to.

### 4.3.5   Evidence From Other Studies

It is interesting that earlier studies which have included some consideration of why companies lease have not tended to find that tax advantage has been a prime motive. Again, direct comparison cannot be made strictly because of sampling differences and the structure of questions, but nevertheless it is of relevance to examine the results of such studies briefly in relation to this particular characteristic.

Fawthrop and Terry (1975), in their study of debt management and the use of leasing finance, found that companies did not consider tax implications to be particularly relevant in their use of leasing. The question in their study concerning reasons for the past, present and future use of finance leasing together with a summary of responses is shown in Table 4.9.

Not surprisingly, since this study is over ten years old, it was looking at the period before the major rise in leasing took place. This distribution of factors influencing the decision to lease is therefore to be expected to be different. It might give a lead to the relevant characteristics in the future when the great tax incentive no longer exists. However, the surprising feature is that leasing as part of a 'planned financing mix' is the emphasised factor, when for our South West survey the results were rather different. Other than that, the

*Table* 4.9  Fawthrop and Terry: Reasons for leasing

*'If your company used, uses or will use leasing, do any or all of the following factors apply?'*

|  | Very relevant | Relevant | Irrelevant |
|---|---|---|---|
| The need was/is/will be urgent, no other funds being available, i.e. leasing is 'emergency financing'. | 7 | 4 | 28 |
| Leasing is part of a 'planned financing mix'. | 17 | 12 | 12 |
| Leasing is 'spill-over' financing, i.e. covers deficiencies or shortfalls in planning. | 7 | 6 | 25 |
| Leasing is 'off-balance sheet' financing and so:<br>(a) Does not affect borrowing capacity. | 8 | 15 | 18 |
| (b) Improves the apparent return on capital employed. | 4 | 14 | 19 |
| Because your company has very large capital allowances, any new equipment would be unable to benefit fully from the 100% first-year relief and so leasing was used as an alternative. | 8 | 5 | 25 |

*Source*:  Fawthrop and Terry (1975) Q.8, p. 305.

survey gives some support for each of the hypotheses, but does not distinguish sharply amongst them.

In a similar study in the following year, Sykes (1976) examined leasing practice in 202 BIM member companies. The advantages of leasing as a source of funds and the budgetary advantages of leasing are shown in Tables 4.10 and 4.11 respectively. The great advantage of this work is that it permits a contrast of the relative advantages of finance leasing, operating leasing and hire purchase. Having said that, the percentage answers to most questions, where applicable, are not very different from these methods.

What stands out from Table 4.10 is that all three methods are

*Table* 4.10   Sykes: Advantages of leasing (% managers)

*Advantages of leasing as a source of funds*

| | Advantages of: | | |
| --- | --- | --- | --- |
| | *Hire purchase (N = 193)* | *Operating leases (N = 185)* | *Finance leases (N = 175)* |
| Provides source of funds – does not utilise existing working capital. | 67 | 76 | 67 |
| Usually permits 100% financing – full cost of asset can normally be borrowed, secured only on that asset. | 23 | 37 | 29 |
| Less restrictive source of finance – no dilution of equity, no dependence on solvency. | 22 | 28 | 22 |
| Undisclosed source of finance – gearing effectively increased without disclosure on balance sheet. | – | 29 | 23 |
| Reduced capital involvement – maximum potential loss reduced, as lease can be terminated prematurely. | – | 21 | 23 |

*Source*:   Sykes (1976), table 11, p. 20.

thought to provide an additional source of funds. Sykes adds the consideration that the risk of maximum loss is less for leasing as an agreement can be terminated. However, penalty clauses usually make that a rather unattractive option.

The results in Table 4.11 show the importance generally given by lessees to the cash flow effects of leasing. In an attempt to examine the extent to which the tax implications of leasing are realised, Sykes suggested to respondents that: 'If the taxable profits of an asset user were insufficient for him to benefit from the full capital allowance on the purchase of an asset in the first year, it might benefit him to lease the asset from a lessor who is able to make immediate use of the tax allowance', and then asked, 'How important is consideration of this factor to you?' The results are given in Table 4.12.

Although 54 per cent of managers who committed themselves to an opinion (this figure excludes 13 per cent of the total sample who were undecided or did not answer the question) indicated an awareness of tax implications, 65 per cent of the number answering felt that the

*Table* 4.11   Sykes: Advantages of leasing (% managers)

*The budgetary advantages of leasing*

| | Hire purchase (N=193) | Advantages of: Operating leases (N=185) | Finance leases (N=175) |
|---|---|---|---|
| Smoothes cash flow. | 45 | 48 | 41 |
| Hedge against inflation – removes problems of possible increase in interest rates. | 19 | 22 | 17 |
| Budgetary accuracy. | 17 | 21 | 22 |
| Stability – terms independent of market conditions or changes in government policy. | 15 | 17 | 15 |
| Flexibility of contract – may be drawn up to suit the needs of the lessee, e.g. repayments timed to suit cash flows. | – | 30 | 21 |

*Source*:   Sykes (1976), table 12, p. 21.

*Table* 4.12   Sykes: Tax implications (% companies) (N=193)

*The importance of immediate availability of tax allowance when leasing equipment*

| | |
|---|---|
| Vitally important | 7 |
| Important | 19 |
| Undecided | 9 |
| Relatively unimportant | 34 |
| Totally unimportant | 31 |
| | 100 |

*Source*:   Sykes (1976), table 13, p. 25.

immediate availability of tax allowances through leasing to be relatively or totally unimportant. However, 25 per cent of managers who committed themselves to an answer gave reasons why tax advantage was unimportant. In general, it was thought that taxable profits were unlikely to be sufficient to absorb capital allowance or, if this did occur, group relief could be utilised. Further analysis by Sykes

*Table* 4.13   Tomkins, Lowe and Morgan: Reasons for leasing

*Why small company lessees are leasing*

| | | Average Points | |
| Reason | Operating leasing | Financial leasing | All leasing |
|---|---|---|---|
| 1  No large capital outlay | 75.9 | 50.0 | 71.5 |
| 2  Asset not on balance sheet | 2.5 | | 2.4 |
| 3  Savings on administration of assets | 1.6 | | 1.5 |
| 4  Stabilised financing arrangements | 1.6 | | 1.5 |
| 5  Taxation advantage | 3.1 | | 2.9 |
| 6  Other | 15.3 | 50.0 | 20.3 |
| Total | 100.0 | 100.0 | 100.0 |
| Number of lessees | 16 | 2 | 17* |

* One company used financial and operating leasing:
*Source*:   Tomkins, Lowe and Morgan (1979), table 8.4, p. 94.

showed the importance of tax advantage to large companies. All the companies with an annual turnover of over £100 million gave an opinion and of these almost half of them considered tax allowanced important. Nevertheless, even this when compared with the NIESR sample shows that perceptions have changed very substantially over the last ten years.

More recently, in their investigation of the significance of leasing to small firms, Tomkins, Lowe and Morgan (1979) included a question intended to gain some indication of why small companies lease. This is probably the most comparable study to our own survey of firms in the South West. A system of allocating 100 points over a number of reasons to indicate the relative importance of each was used. The total number for each reason was then divided by the number of lessees. The results are shown in Table 4.13. Only two companies had used finance leasing and the authors commented that 'the reasons given for leasing yielded the expected conclusion of little tax-based leasing for small companies'. Most firms indicated that leasing avoided large capital outlay and from comments made by most of the respondents it would seem that there was no other available source of finance at the time. With such small use of leasing revealed, this really does not provide a very good basis for us to form further judgements on the basis to proceed.

*Table* 4.14   Hull and Hubbard: Reasons for using finance leasing

|  | Important factor | Marginal factor |
|---|---|---|
| Conserved cash flow | 54% | 24% |
| Cheaper than purchase | 45% | 19% |
| Additional form of finance which does not affect other borrowing sources | 27% | 26% |
| Assisted in having a mixed financial strategy | 22% | 27% |
| Safeguard against obsolescence | 18% | 19% |
| Certainty of fixed payments | 12% | 31% |

*Source*:   Hull and Hubbard (1980), p. 628.

In the only other relevant previous study which we considered, Hull and Hubbard (1980) examined the attitudes and behaviour of lessees in the UK leasing industry. The main reasons why companies in their sample used finance leasing are shown in Table 4.14. It is clear from the results that, as the authors themselves conclude, 'not all lessees are leasing for tax related reasons'.[3] Again, cash flow comes out at the top of the list, this time closely followed by cost, but the addition to sources of finance comes some way behind as the third most important factor. There is thus a communality in these studies and a general emphasis on a smaller role for tax-based leasing than our results so far seem to show.

Further evidence of this was provided in their study by the fact that only 16 per cent of companies referred to tax in replying to a question on company policy regarding whether and when to lease equipment. In addition, the survey also fund that 48 per cent of companies which had been liable to tax over the previous two years had in fact also leased assets during that period. The corresponding figure for leasing by companies which had not been taxpayers over the same period was 59 per cent.

It is evident that each of these previous studies of why lessees lease suggests that companies may lease for a number of reasons and that the decision to lease is not wholly dependent upon tax considerations. Fawthrop and Terry (1975) found that leasing as part of a 'planned financial mix' was particularly relevant to major corporations. Sykes' (1976) survey indicated that reasons related to cash flow (i.e. 'provides source of funds – does not utilise existing working capital' and 'smoothes cash flow') were considered important advantages by lessees and that, although many managers were aware of tax implications, the majority felt that they were unimportant. Tomkins, Lowe and Morgan (1979) showed that the avoidance of large capital outlay and the fact that there was simply no other source of finance available was significant to small companies. Finally, Hull and Hubbard (1980) concluded from their study that the rationale for leasing is not totally based on tax advantage and that conservation of cash flow had been a most important factor. Our survey has shown that tax advantage would seem to be more important to the generally larger companies from the NIESR survey panel, rather than to those in the South West survey where the avoidance of large capital outlay tended to be more marked as a factor taken into account when deciding to lease.

The emphasis placed by lessees on cash flow is interesting. Hubbard (1980 B) has demonstrated that there is no cash flow advantage to leasing before or after tax if leasing is compared with a loan of equivalent interest cost and comparable repayment schedule, except in instances where leasing is cheaper than borrowing or if a comparable loan cannot be obtained. Hubbard gives as an example the situation where a company is unable to obtain further bank finance. We have seen that this position was noted in the study of the signicance of leasing to small companies by Tomkins, Lowe and Morgan (1979), and indeed in the present survey a number of respondents in the South West survey referred to a lack of alternative funds when using leasing. However, this position will obviously not apply to all companies, particularly larger organisations with corporate treasury departments, and the relative cost of leasing will therefore be an important determinant of cash flow advantage. It is arguable that some respondents may not have fully appreciated the tax advantage of leasing and identified cash flow as being more important, whereas in fact there might be a causal relationship between the two factors.

### 4.3.6  Reasons for Not Using Leasing

In addition to considering the reasons why companies lease, a further question was included in our own surveys to try to determine why companies which had not used leasing had made that decision, and, in particular, to explore the extent to which non-use was related to the ability of companies to benefit directly from capital allowances. Of the 138 non-lessee companies in the South West survey, ninety-seven had considered using leasing, while in the NIESR survey, two

*Table* 4.15   Factors taken into account when deciding not to lease

|  | SOUTH WEST ECONOMIC PLANNING REGION *Number of responses* | NIESR *Number of responses* |
|---|---|---|
| Too expensive compared to other sources of funds | 37 | 2 |
| Asset did not qualify for capital allowances | 8 | 0 |
| Prefer to own assets | 50 | 0 |
| Able to take direct advantage of capital allowances | 47 | 2 |
| Other | 4 | 0 |

of four non-lessee companies had considered using leasing. A summary of responses for each sample of the factors taken into account when deciding not to lease is given in Table 4.15.

In the South West sample there is quite a marked preference towards ownership of assets rather than leasing. However, a large number of companies have indicated that they were able to take direct advantage of capital allowances or that leasing was too expensive compared to other sources of funds. It is interesting that both categories attracted proportionately large numbers of responses because firms will tend to find leasing expensive if they are able to utilise capital allowances immediately. There is, of course, no one leasing rate, in the same way that there is no one cost of alternative finance. Relative costs will be affected by the position of companies, their plans and the nature of the assets they want to acquire. It is therefore quite possible to find companies which are in the situations described.

Both Tomkins, Lowe and Morgan (1979) and Hull and Hubbard (1980) also tried to find out why companies did not lease. The results that Tomkins, Lowe and Morgan (1979) obtained from their questions are shown in Table 4.16.

Most firms replied that they did not use leasing because their investment was limited and could be financed from other sources. It is noticeable that the cost of leasing was also an important consideration.

*Table* 4.16   Tomkins, Lowe and Morgan: Reasons for not leasing

*Why some small companies do not lease*

| Reason | Non quoted | Average points Eventually quoted | Total |
|---|---|---|---|
| 1  Did not think of it | 3.1 | – | 0.7 |
| 2  Aware of existence of leasing but no ready information | 3.1 | 1.0 | 1.5 |
| 3  Leasing was too expensive | 31.2 | 25.4 | 26.8 |
| 4  Local bank manager more sympathetic in difficult times | 3.1 | 10.4 | 8.7 |
| 5  Other | 59.4 | 68.2 | 62.3 |
| | 100.0 | 100.0 | 100.0 |
| Number of companies responding | 16 | 5 | 167 |

*Source:*   Tomkins, Lowe and Morgan (1979), table 8.5, p. 96.

*Table* 4.17   Hull and Hubbard: Reasons for not using finance leasing

| | Number of responses |
|---|---|
| Lack of awareness | 1 |
| More expensive than alternatives | 59 |
| Some key executives opposed to leasing | 15 |
| Fixed commitment leads to a loss of flexibility | 6 |
| Understates assets on balance sheet | 7 |
| Lack of eligibility for government incentives | 8 |
| Incompatible with company's image | 7 |
| Other (specify): | |
| Not group policy | 7 |

*Source*:   Hull and Hubbard (1980), Q.26, p. 111.

However, most implied that they had considered leasing as a possibility.

Similar results were obtained by Hull and Hubbard in their survey, as is shown in Table 4.17. Leasing simply appeared more expensive than the alternative sources of funds, which in itself tells us something about the position of these firms.

In a further question concerning why companies considered leasing to be more expensive than alternatives, most respondents indicated that either the 'company is in a tax paying position with no shortage

*Table* 4.18   Effect of leasing on the overall quantity of investment undertaken (number (percentage of) companies)

|  | SOUTH WEST ECONOMIC PLANNING REGION | NIESR |
|---|---|---|
| Increased | 59   (22.0) | 2    (7.7) |
| Remained unaltered | 200   (74.6) | 24   (92.3) |
| Decreased | 6    (2.3) | 0    (0.0) |
| Not specified | 3    (1.1) | – |
| Total | 268 (100.0) | 26 (100.0) |

of funds' or 'leasing costs include lessor's costs and profit which are not included in alternatives'.

It is clear that the non-use of leasing is affected by firms' ability to take immediate advantage of capital allowances and the cost of leasing. As we have seen, these factors are interrelated and arise from the taxpaying position of the firm.

## 4.4   EFFECTS ON THE QUANTITY AND TIMING OF INVESTMENT

Since the primary objective of the present study is the examination of how leasing has affected the level and timing of investment expenditures, we sought firms' opinions on both these factors to determine the perceived effects of leasing at the microeconomic level. The result for both samples on how leasing has affected the overall quantity of investment undertaken by respondent lessees is shown in Table 4.18. It is immediately evident that most firms considered that the overall quantity of investment has remained unaltered – 74.6 per cent in the South West sample and 92.3 per cent in the NIESR survey panel sample. A number of firms offered explanations as to why this was considered the case. In the South West survey some firms suggested that leasing had no impact on the quantity of investment because its use was limited (often to equipment peripheral to the main business activity). Others indicated that the reason why investment had not been affected arose from the investment decision-making process showing that the investment and financing decisions are taken separately. For example, one respondent commented that 'the decision to invest was taken and then the method of finance decided', whilst another asserted 'leasing only affects the financing decision – not whether an asset is procured or not'. This is most interesting as Fawthrop and Terry (1976) have argued that the leasing decision cannot be taken in isolation from the investment decision, and that the decision to lease is a simultaneous investment and financing decision as a result of differing tax costs and benefits associated with leasing and ownership financing. It is evident from comments made (e.g. 'decisions on capital investment have been made on the merits of the project. Finance could be provided either through leasing or bank overdraft. Leasing has been cheaper due to tax advantages' or 'the project justification procedure is not significantly influenced by varying methods of finance') that this is not necessarily appreciated by businessmen. In many cases it was felt that investment was determined by operational requirements and would have taken place whether leasing was available or not.

Similar observations were made by firms on the NIESR survey panel (e.g. 'to lease or not is a financing decision and as such has no bearing on the capital expenditure decision' or the 'decision to lease . . . [is] . . . made independently after project appraisal').

From the comments made by those respondents who indicated that leasing had increased their level of investment, it is clear that the effect of leasing on investment was not thought to be solely dependent upon the tax mechanism. In the South West survey firms identified the following causal factors:

— capital saving;
— investment decision made simpler;
— cash flow;
— lack of alternative funds;
— specific assets (i.e. computers) would not have been otherwise acquired;
— tax advantages reflected in the cost of finance;
— off-balance sheet advantages.

Of these factors, reference to the lack of alternative sources of funds and capital savings were most common. Only two firms in the NIESR survey considered that leasing had increased investment and of these one identified 'increased availability of funds and ability to match capital outlay with anticipated revenues', whilst the other explained that 'leasing allowed expenditure to be excluded from the balance sheet and reduced debt. Financing costs were lower because tax leases were used.'

We also asked respondents to try to quantify the effect of leasing in increasing the level of investment. In the South West survey many firms indicated percentage rises which ranged from 5 per cent to 150 per cent, whilst monetary estimates extended from £20 000 per annum to £2 million over a five year period. The estimates given by the two firms from the NIESR survey were an increase of £1/3 and 5–10 million per annum. Although these figures are difficult to assess in isolation, it is nevertheless evident that the effect has not been negligible. There is, however, no clear basis on which any aggregation would be made for the economy as a whole. The effects of leasing on the timing of investment as identified by lessees followed a broadly similar pattern to those on the quantity, with the majority of respondents from both samples indicating that timing had remained unaltered. The results are shown in Table 4.19.

In the South West survey firms suggested that capital investment was determined by operational requirements and formed part of the corporate planning structure so that leasing had little effect on timing. Other comments referred to the separation of the investment and financing decisions and the fact that alternative sources of finance had been available. Firms from the NIESR panel indicated that investment decisions are principally determined by the market and not by the means of finance. Again, emphasis was laid on the secondary nature of financing in the investment process.

Firms that considered investment had been brought forward in time by leasing gave a number of reasons. In the South West survey the lack of available funds, cash flow and tax advantages were

*Table* 4.19   Effect of leasing on the timing of investment (number (percentage of) companies)

|  | SOUTH WEST ECONOMIC PLANNING REGION | NIESR |
|---|---|---|
| Been brought forward | 56   (20.9) | 2   (7.7) |
| Remained unaltered | 202   (75.4) | 24   (92.3) |
| Been delayed | 2   (0.7) | 0   (0.0) |
| Not specified | 8   (3.0) |  |
| Total | 268   (100.0) | 26   (100.0) |

identified with time periods ranging from 3–4 months to 2 years. Of the two respondents from the NIESR survey panel that indicated a positive influence, one suggested that investment had been brought forward by $1\frac{1}{2}$ years as a result of the relative cost of funding and the other commented that following the 1984 Budget there had been a limited 'pull-forward' of capital expenditures between quarters.

The results of both the effects of leasing on the quantity and timing of investment are of interest. First, they suggest that the effects are working at the margin. Although this at first sight might indicate that leasing has had very little impact on investment at the microeconomic level, for the economy as a whole the effect may well be significant. After all, if 20 per cent of firms have increased investment and a similar percentage have brought forward investment as a result of leasing, even if this were only a small portion of their own investment this is still a noticeable affect on total investment. Second, although tax advantage has been taken into account by many firms in deciding to lease, this cost of finance advantage has not been directly associated with the investment decision. This is perhaps not surprising in the case of smaller firms where the mere availability of finance has been an important consideration. However, it would appear that by separating the investment and financing decisions firms may not fully reflect the impact of leasing on investment.

## 4.5   SALES-AID LEASING

In addition to its direct effects on investment, leasing may also influence the sales of firms and thereby the level of investment through its use as a sales-aid. The survey included questions designed to obtain information on the extent of sales-aid activity, how the facility has been provided and its perceived effects on the level and timing of sales to customers. In the South West survey thirty–six respondent companies offered sales-aid leasing and six companies from the NIESR survey panel were engaged in this type of activity. Methods of sales-aid leasing range from simple referral to a finance company to the operation of 'in house' leasing facilities. The methods used by the companies are shown in Table 4.20.

Most companies have provided sales-aid leasing through finance companies, although it is evident that 'in house' facilities have been used to a certain extent. The employment of lease brokers does not appear to be widespread.

*Table* 4.20   Methods of sales-aid leasing used (number companies)

|  | SOUTH WEST ECONOMIC PLANNING REGION | NIESR |
|---|---|---|
| Through a finance company | 26 | 5 |
| Through a lease broker | 1 | 0 |
| Through own finance company or division | 8 | 3 |
| Other | 3 | 0 |

*Table* 4.21   Effects of sales-aid leasing on customer sales (number (percentage of) companies)

|  | SOUTH WEST ECONOMIC PLANNING REGION | NIESR |
|---|---|---|
| Increased | 15   (41.7) | 3   (50.0) |
| Remained unaltered | 17   (47.2) | 2   (33.3) |
| Not specified | 4   (11.1) | 1   (16.7) |
| Totals | 36 (100.0) | 6 (100.0) |

In contrast to direct effects on investment, the use of leasing as a sales-aid would seem to have a significant impact on the South West survey, both in terms of the quantity of sales to customers and the timing of sales. Table 4.21 shows that although seventeen (53.1 per cent of those companies that specified an effect) indicated that the quantity of sales had remained unaltered, fifteen companies (46.9 per cent) suggested that sales had increased. However, if leasing generally had no effect on sales one would ask why companies bothered to do it as it would not be a 'sales-aid'.

In examining the results of companies from the NIESR survey panel there is clearly a problem of dealing with very small numbers of respondents. Three companies indicate an increase while two consider that the quantity has remained unaltered – similar proportions to the South West survey.

Again, the effect of timing was quite marked in the South West survey. Table 4.22 indicates that of those companies specifying an effect, eighteen companies (58.9 per cent) felt that the timing of customers' decisions to purchase had remained unaltered, while

*Table* 4.22   Effect of sales-aid leasing on the timing of customers' decisions to purchase (number (percentage of) companies)

|  | SOUTH WEST ECONOMIC PLANNING REGION | NIESR |
|---|---|---|
| Been brought forward | 13 (36.1) | 1 (16.7) |
| Remained unaltered | 18 (50.0) | 4 (66.6) |
| Not specified | 5 (13.9) | 1 (16.7) |
| Totals | 36 (100.0) | 6 (100.0) |

thirteen (41.9 per cent) thought that they had been brought forward. Table 4.22 shows that only one company considered that timing had been brought forward from the NIESR panel, but four thought that it had remained unaltered. These figures, of course, do not tell us how far forward or what proportion of any firm's sales was brought forward.

## 4.6   THE EFFECTS OF THE 1984 FINANCE ACT

The 1984 Budget has fundamentally affected the nature of the leasing market. Questions were inserted into the survey in an attempt to form an assessment of the effects of changes in rates of corporate taxation and capital allowances, both in the interim period since the Budget and also for the position after March 1986 by which time first-year allowances will have largely been phased out. The effects of the 1984 Budget up to the time of the survey (i.e. April 1984 to September/October 1985) are shown in Table 4.23.

The results show that in both samples for the majority of firms the amount of leasing undertaken since the Budget has either remained unaltered or decreased. This is perhaps somewhat curious in view of the attractive leasing rates that have been available in this period and the general upsurge in leasing that has been observed in the economy. We have two interpretations of this: first, that firms may not have understood the question fully and may have treated it as a general longer term response, in which case falls in investment are to be expected as the incentive is reduced. The second is, however, that since we were asking at an early stage, firms may not yet have

*Table* 4.23　Effect of 1984 Budget on amount of leasing undertaken (number (percentage of) companies)

|  | SOUTH WEST ECONOMIC PLANNING REGION | NIESR PANEL |
|---|---|---|
| Increased | 50　(18.7) | 2　(7.7) |
| Remained unaltered | 150　(56.0) | 12　(46.2) |
| Decreased | 58　(21.6) | 11　(42.3) |
| Not specified | 10　(3.7) | 1　(3.8) |
| Totals | 268 (100.0) | 26 (100.0) |

*Table* 4.24　Use of leasing after March 1986 (number (percentage of) companies)

|  | SOUTH WEST ECONOMIC PLANNING REGION | NIESR PANEL |
|---|---|---|
| Use more operating leasing than finance leasing | 43　(16.1) | 5　(19.2) |
| Use more finance leasing than operating leasing | 59　(22.0) | 2　(7.7) |
| Use other forms of finance instead | 88　(32.8) | 13　(50.0) |
| Not specified | 78　(29.1) | 6　(23.1) |
| Total | 268 (100.0) | 26 (100.0) |

appreciated that, comparing one year with another, in the two year transition period, it would pay to bring investment forward. We are reluctant, though, to reject answers to one question purely because it conflicts with other evidence, because other answers, which appear to agree with other evidence, may be equally incorrect. It is important to take an unbiased view. That said, this particular set of responses do seem anomalous.

Extending the picture forward, Table 4.24 shows the future use of leasing by expected respondents after March 1986.

Many of those firms that did not specify an alternative indicated that they were undecided at the time of the survey. As might be expected, there is a marked move away from leasing, particularly amongst firms from the NIESR survey panel. In the NIESR survey there is quite a strong movement towards operating leasing but this is not paralled in the South West survey where the continued use of finance leasing is relatively marked. This suggests that firms are leasing for reasons other than tax or that the full implications of the Budget have not been understood. In any event, it would appear that falls in leasing of more than perhaps a half would be surprising in the light of the responses, but equally that substantial reductions are to be expected on the basis of these opinions.


## 4.7   IMPLICATIONS

The questionnaire survey has produced some interesting results concerning the leasing behaviour of firms and its effects upon investment. In particular, it has provided a clear indication that tax advantage is not necessarily considered by firms to be a prime motivation to lease and this may well be related to size of company. In the South West survey, which was largely comprised of smaller firms, avoiding large capital outlay appeared to be the most significant factor in the decision to lease, although many firms did in fact indicate tax advantage, whereas tax advantage was clearly a predominant factor to the firms from the NIESR survey panel which were generally larger. This suggests that leasing may seem attractive to smaller firms, not only as a result of tax-based cost factors, but also in terms of its perceived impact upon cash flow and ultimately because of the lack of alternative sources of finance. It might be expected that larger firms with a range of funding options and perhaps more sophisticated appraisal methods would identify and utilise tax advantage more readily, as is reflected in the rental structure of leasing agreements.

The effects of leasing on investment identified in the survey work are also of interest. It is clear from both samples that most lessees considered that leasing had affected neither the quantity of investment undertaken nor its timing. Thus, at first sight the effects seem to be quite small and, furthermore, the survey indicates that these are not limited to the tax mechanism alone. However, again following Eisner (1957), care should be taken in interpreting these results as a consequence of difficulties in applying survey techniques to investment behaviour and particularly to 'avoid what may be called a public opinion poll mentality which would decide issues of economic theory by a meaningless majority vote'.[4] For such influences, although apparently quite small at the microeconomic level, may well be important in the determination of aggregate investment. We shall return to this point when discussing surveys of the effects of investment incentives on firms' behaviour in the next chapter, which considers leasing and capital formation in the economy as a whole.

# 5 Leasing and the Incentive to Invest

The determinants of capital investment have long been an area of interest both to economists and to policy-makers because of their role in relation to cyclical fluctuations in economic activity and growth of the economy.

The surveys of lessors and lessees at the micro level have suggested that leasing may have important macroeconomic effects on the UK economy. In the principal hypotheses being examined in this study, it has been argued that leasing has not only increased the level of investment rather than merely displacing other forms of finance but has also acted as a counter-cyclical influence in the economy during periods of recession. Much of this effect has occured through the exploitation of lessor's tax allowances for the benefit of lessees who were otherwise tax exhausted.

As previously indicated, the leasing industry has become an increasingly important source of fixed investment. This is illustrated in Table 5.1 which shows the contribution of leased assets to capital expenditure in the UK over the period 1975 to 1985.

The principal hypotheses emphasise the role of imbalance in the system of tax investment incentives in determining the impact of leasing on the economy. A primary purpose of tax investment incentives is to alter the relative price of capital as an inducement to firms to increase their level of investment. This is rather a broad policy instrument aimed at increasing the quantity of investment and is based on the assumption that investment *per se* is desirable and advantageous to the economy. If this is the case, and tax incentives are effective in raising investment levels, then consequently it will be detrimental to the economy when a significant proportion of firms are unable to absorb tax allowances immediately. If tax allowances cannot be used immediately then their value will decline over time. As we have already seen, as a result of expansion in tax reliefs and allowances, a growing number of firms from the mid 1970s, particularly those with large investment programmes, have experienced tax exhaustion. Leasing, which has enabled the lessor to take advantage of capital allowances and to reflect at least some of the tax gain in reduced rentals, has provided tax exhausted firms with a means of

*Table* 5.1   UK fixed capital expenditure and expenditure on assets for leasing (pounds million at 1980 prices)

*Total SIC (1980)*

| Year | Divisions 1–8[1] | All leasing and hiring[2] | Leasing/Total %[3] |
|------|------------------|----------------------------|---------------------|
| 1975 | 23176 | 1006 | 4.3 |
| 1976 | 23593 | 1112 | 4.7 |
| 1977 | 24000 | 1396 | 5.8 |
| 1978 | 25400 | 2012 | 7.9 |
| 1979 | 26410 | 2647 | 10.0 |
| 1980 | 25370 | 2873 | 11.3 |
| 1981 | 23521 | 3005 | 12.8 |
| 1982 | 24037 | 3341 | 13.9 |
| 1983 | 24354 | 3294 | 13.5 |
| 1984 | 26823 | 3936 | 14.7 |
| 1985 | 27706 | 4864 | 17.6 |

[1] Includes preliminary fourth quarter projections for SIC Divisions 1–7.
[2] Comprising finance leasing and SIC Class 84 (Operational Leasing and Hiring).
[3] (All Leasing and Hiring/SIC Divisions 1–8) × 100.
*Source*:   Business Statistics Office.

indirectly obtaining immediate benefit from such investment incentives. It is largely through this mechanism that we have argued that leasing has led to investment which might not otherwise have taken place.

Given the emphasis placed on tax investment incentives as an instrument of economic policy and their role in relation to leasing, it is therefore clearly an important part of the present study to examine evidence of the effects that such incentives have had on investment behaviour in general, to contrast them with other incentives to invest, and to consider their effectiveness in the context of the leasing transaction.

## 5.1   TAX INCENTIVES FOR INVESTMENT IN THE UK

Since the war governments have used both tax investment incentives and direct investment grants to influence the level of investment in the economy. Investment incentives operating through the tax system have consisted of initial allowances and investment allowances. An initial allowance is a form of accelerated depreciation which permits the firm to write off a proportion of the cost of an asset in the first year at a rate above the normal depreciation rate allowed for tax purposes (the annual writing-down allowance). However, although depreciation is accelerated initially, it is amended accordingly in subsequent years so as not to exceed the cost of the asset. By accelerating depreciation payment of tax is deferred in proportion to the quantity of investment undertaken. This is clearly advantageous to the investing firm, especially in periods of rapid inflation, and the initial allowance is commonly likened to a temporary interest free loan. An investment allowance is similar in operation to the initial allowance in that it enables the firm to write off a proportion of the cost of an asset immediately in addition to the normal tax depreciation rate, but differs because subsequent depreciation remains unaltered. In the case of investment allowances, therefore, taxation is both deferred and reduced as a consequence of the allowance being applied over and above normal depreciation. It is in effect a subsidy on investment and can be regarded as a form of 'grant' working through the tax system rather than by direct payment. An investment grant is simply a cash grant made to firms by the government to subsidise capital expenditure.

In the period since 1945, when initial allowances were first introduced, there have been several changes in the rate and type of incentive available to firms. Table 5.2 shows statutory grants and allowances for plant and machinery capital expenditure by manufacturing industry in the period 1945 to 1972 when 100 per cent first-year allowances were introduced.

Initial allowances and investment allowances have been used both separately and in conjunction with one another, withdrawn and reintroduced at various points in time. Investment grants have been introduced and subsequently withdrawn. In addition, investment incentives have varied between regions and also types of asset. The following discussion is primarily concerned with those incentives that have been available to all firms in the economy irrespective of location and specific assistance.

## 5.2　HOW TAX INCENTIVES ENCOURAGE INVESTMENT

Investment incentives are considered to encourage investment by firms in a number of ways. The cost of investment is reduced directly by cash investment grants and indirectly through the system of

Table 5.2  Statutory grants and allowances for plant and machinery capital expenditure by manufacturing industry

| Announcement date | National | | | | Development areas | |
|---|---|---|---|---|---|---|
| | Investment allowances % | Initial allowances % | Writing down allowances % | Grants[1] % | Initial allowances % | Grants[2] % |
| 24.4.45 | 0 | 20 | 15.3 | | | |
| 6.4.49 | 0 | 40 | 15.3 | | | |
| 10.4.51 | 0 | 0 | 15.3 | | | |
| 15.4.53 | 0 | 20 | 15.3 | | | |
| 6.4.54 | 20 | 0 | 15.3 | | | |
| 17.2.56 | 0 | 20 | 15.3 | | | |
| 15.4.58 | 0 | 25 | 15.3 | | | |
| 17.6.58 | 0 | 30 | 15.3 | | | |
| 7.4.59 | 20 | 10 | 15.3 | | | |
| 5.11.62 | 30 | 10 | 20 | | | |
| 3.4.63 | 30 | 10 | 20 | | | |
| 17.1.66 | | | 20 | 20 | 100 | 10 |
| 1.12.66* | | | 20 | 25 | | 40 |
| 1.1.69* | | | 20 | 20 | | 45 |
| 27.10.70 | | 35 | 25 | | 100 | 40 |
| 19.7.71+ | | 55 | 25 | | 100 | |
| 21.3.72 | | 100 | | | 100 | 20++ |

Notes:
[1] These are based on a number of rates varying according to type of asset up to 1966.
[2] No account has been taken of schemes for intermediate and special development areas or discretionary assistance made available under Section 7 of the 1972 Industry Act.
* The temporary grant increase of 1.12.66 was announced to be limited to expenditure between 1.1.67 and 31.12.68. 1.1.69 therefore refers to the date on which grants actually reverted to their previous levels.
+ It was announced that this change would be of a limited duration applying to expenditure made before 1.8.73.
++ 1972 Regional Development Grants do not reduce the value of capital expenditure qualifying for tax allowances.
Source:  Melliss and Richardson (1976), table 2, p. 32.

taxation. It is generally held that investment incentives can affect firms' investment behaviour by their impact on liquidity and profitability. The 'liquidity effect' arises from those incentives which strengthen the cash flow position of the firm after the investment has taken place. The income generated by investment only accrues with a lag, after the investment starts contributing to the production process. Hence funds need to be raised and financed initially until the inflow of income enables them to be repaid. Any investment incentive which improves the cash flow position during that period will clearly make it easier to invest. Cash flow will determine the level of internal funds available to the firm which itself has historically been an important source of investment finance.

The 'profitability effect' results from incentives which change the time profile of tax payments or actually reduce payment of tax and improve the after-tax return on investment. Although there has long been considerable debate over the precise determinants of investment both liquidity and profitability have been thought to be important.

Existing studies of the effectiveness of investment incentives have broadly taken two forms – those that have relied on the use of survey (questionnaire and interview) techniques, and those that have employed econometric modelling to analyse the role and significance of incentives in the investment process.

## 5.3   EVIDENCE FROM SAMPLE SURVEYS

Several surveys of investment behaviour and the effects of incentives have been undertaken in the post-war period. The result of such surveys have tended to vary quite considerably. Some have shown investment incentives to have a relatively limited impact on the investment behaviour of firms whilst others have indicated a more important role.

Many of the studies carried out in the late 1950s and early 1960s did not find evidence that firms' investment behaviour was significantly affected by the presence of investment incentives. In providing evidence to the Radcliffe Committee on the Working of the Monetary System, a postal survey of its members conducted by the Federation of British Industry (1957) contained questions about the effect of changes in investment and initial allowances on firms' investment decisions. It was found that of 1595 respondent firms, only 23 per cent indicated that their investment decisions had been materially affected by favourable changes, whereas the investment decisions of 14 per cent had been affected by unfavourable changes in allowances.

In a much smaller study carried out by Hart and Prussman (1964) as part of an investigation into management accounting techniques in firms in the South-East Hampshire area, a considerably wider impact of allowances was reported. The authors sought information whether 'investment allowances for plant and machinery (for taxation purposes)[had] at any time proved to be an inducement [to firms] to replace (or add to) plant and machinery'. Replies to the questionnaire were received from 116 firms and of these forty-two said investment allowances had in fact been an inducement to invest.

Similar results were also obtained by Corner and Williams (1965) who undertook a more extensive survey of the sensitivity of business to initial and investment allowances. Their main finding was that of 181 establishments, only twenty-nine were responsive to initial or investment allowances and twenty-nine were responsive to both initial and investment allowances. As with the studies by the Federation of British Industry and Hart and Prussman, this does not suggest that investment incentives played a major role in determining patterns of investment. From the survey, Corner and Williams tentatively concluded that firms which had experienced financial difficulties were slightly more responsive than others; amongst independent businesses, medium and large firms were more responsive than small firms, and growing firms were more responsive than stationary or declining firms. Significantly, it was also concluded that the 'liquidity effect' of allowances seemed to be somewhat more important than the 'profitability effect'.

Unfortunately, much of the evidence which has been accumulated over the years has been from relatively small studies with a limited coverage. A National Economic Development Council (1965) survey examined the interaction of tax concessions and investment decisions. It was found that fifty-seven of sixty companies indicated that tax concessions had no direct effect on investment decisions. However, sixteen companies considered that tax concessions were a positive influence on cash flow. Of these, nine indicated that they were reasonably certain that such concessions had been instrumental in increasing their level of investment above that which it would otherwise have been, whilst seven said that concessions might have been instrumental. These findings at first sight appear to be contradictory. Lund (1971, p. 83) has explained this by suggesting that the term 'direct effect' was interpreted by respondent firms as relating to the 'profitability effect' whereas 'aid to cash flow' refered to the 'liquidity effect'. If this is a correct interpretation, then it would broadly concur with the conclusions of Corner and Williams on the relative influence of these effects.

In contrast, other surveys undertaken in the 1960s and 1970s found that investment incentives had a more positive effect on investment decisions. In a questionnaire survey carried out by the Confederation of British Industry (1965), approximately 66 per cent of 438 respondent firms (which had undertaken almost half of the gross fixed investment of manufacturing industry in the period 1962 to 1964) allowed for the effects of investment incentives in their cash flow analysis. This figure rose quite dramatically to 93 per cent when taking into account those firms with an annual investment expenditure of over £1/2 million. Over 25 per cent of the firms confirmed that investment decisions had been affected by the presence of or changes in the rate of investment allowances. However, it is worth emphasising at this point that subsequent studies have also indicated that the sheer number and frequency of changes in the investment incentive system had acted as a discouragement to firms, as they would not be certain of the rates which apply when their plans came to fruition.

George (1968), in an examination of productivity and capital expenditure in retailing, also found evidence of more substantial effects of investment incentives on capital expenditure. From a total of eighty-four firms, thirty-five said investment allowances had an effect on investment decisions. However, only seven of the thirty-five firms were able to provide specific instances where investment incentives were a crucial factor in the decision-making process. Reasons given why investment incentives were not thought to be of importance included uncertainity in respect of turnover and adequate liquidity.

A Ministry of Technology (1970) *Investment Incentives Survey*, using both questionnaire and interview techniques, provided further evidence that a significant number of firms were sensitive to investment incentives. A total of 300 firms were sent questionnaires to which some 40 per cent replied. Of the 300 firms, including those that did not reply to the questionnaire, forty-five were subsequently interviewed. Interviews were also conducted with a small number of other firms. Taking into account the data from both the questionnaire survey and the interviews, it was possible to conclude that about one-third of the firms included the effects of capital allowances in investment appraisal whilst two-thirds allowed for investment grants.

It was also found that firms which accounted for 94 per cent of the investment of those which took part in the interviews were sensitive to changes in incentives. Further analysis showed that in terms of the manner in which the effects of both grants and allowances had an impact on the investment process, those firms which accounted for 62 per cent of total investment undertaken indicated an effect on profitability while the remainder of firms accounting for 32 per cent of investment indicated an effect on liquidity.

It might be thought, therefore, that these studies had provided conclusive evidence for the effect of incentives on investment. However, unlike the studies by the Confederation of British Industry, George and the Ministry of Technology, a survey of the investment policies and practices of sixty-nine companies of various sizes and industrial types by Rockley (1973) indicated that investment patterns by the respondents did not seem to show any definite correlations between the volume of investment and the value of inducements. His findings suggested that the level of demand for firms' products and replacement of worn out equipment were the most common factors leading to investment expenditure. The study concluded that 'taxation reductions and investment grants or allowances may add to the corporate cash flow which may act so as to enable some additional capital expenditures. But ultimately it is the consumers' liquidity which will affect the corporate liquidity and its power to invest'.[1]

More recently, Alam and Stafford (1985) have examined the influence of tax incentives on the investment policies of companies in UK manufacturing industry by postal questionnaire. They also have findings in broad agreement with Rockley and suggest that tax reliefs were not considered by respondents to be one of the more important factors in determining investment policies. Of 130 firms replying to the question – 'What in your view are the most important factors determining the level of investment in your company?' – only 6.2 per cent cited investment allowances and tax savings. Investment decisions appeared to be largely influenced by expected sales, profits and conditions in the economy. However, the survey results did indicate that large firms were more likely to be responsive to taxation and incentives than small firms. The study concluded that whilst tax incentives have some influence on investment decisions for a minority of firms (and that this might not be negligible since it related to large companies), most firms did not appear to be influenced by taxation and incentives.

It is clear that questionnaire and interview surveys of investment behaviour in the UK indicate quite a wide divergence of opinion amongst businessmen concerning the effects of investment incentives. Some of this divergence may be attributable to the timing of individual studies in relation to changes in the type and rate of investment incentive available. In the period from 1945 to the introduction of the 100 per cent first-year allowance, for example, there were some sixteen changes in incentives relating to plant and machinery.[2] A further consideration is that there are a number of methodological difficulties in undertaking studies of this nature. Problems may arise in establishing a representative sampling framework of firms and determining accurately the degree of coverage that can be inferred from respondents. In addition, there are difficulties in formulating questions in such a way as to isolate precisely those particular effects which are being studied. Lund (1971, p. 58) has discussed the limitations of using questionnaire and interview techniques to study investment behaviour in the light of previous work by White (1956) and Eisner (1957). One point of particular relevance to the present study and the results of the survey of the leasing behaviour of firms is examined by Lund. It concerns the relationship between microeconomic surveys and possible macroeconomic implications and merits quotation in full:

Even if interview and questionnaire studies successfully elicit information about the variables which individual firms consider to be important determinants of their investment decisions, they may still not provide much guide to the variables which are important at the macro level. In particular, individual firms are likely to underestimate the effects on aggregate investment of those variables which affect all of them in the same way, such as interest rates and tax allowances to investment.[3]

Surveys may indicate that factors such as tax incentives are of marginal significance to the investment behaviour of the individual firm, but it is possible that at the macroeconomic level they may be of importance if only because the sum of a large number of marginal influences may nevertheless be substantial. Lund therefore asserts that 'the significance of particular variables in the determination of aggregate investment can only be assessed successfully by first formulating econometric models to explain the aggregate, and then subjecting them to appropriate statistical testing'[4] – an area to which we now turn our attention.

## 5.4   ECONOMETRIC EVIDENCE

The role of investment incentives in determining the level of fixed investment has received considerable attention in econometric studies of investment. Our discussion of such studies will be principally concerned with UK studies although a large amount of work in this field has also been undertaken in the USA.[5] It is not intended to present a full survey of the literature but rather to explore some of the results of attempts to assess the impact of incentive in order to form an overview. As with the survey studies of investment incentives, the overall evidence presented by the use of econometric modelling techniques unfortunately tends to be somewhat inconclusive.

An early study by Agarwala and Goodson (1969)[6] suggested that incentives had quite a marked impact on investment. They tested the hypothesis that changes in investment incentives and corporation tax will affect the profitability and/or liquidity of firms and thereby possibly the rate at which investment will occur. The study also sought to estimate the magnitude of the effects of such policies on investment. In their model, investment was determined by the amount of funds available for investment and the rate of return from investment in fixed capital. The model was tested over the period 1958 to 1966 to explain investment intentions and implied that they were significantly influenced by both variables. The effects of investment incentives were examined by varying a number of hypothetical policy measures and determining how such variations affected cash flows (as an indicator of investible funds) and the rate of return. It was found that when a policy measure is changed, the effect is initially to alter the rate of return only, but in the second year both the change in the rate of return and change in cash flows will affect investment. Both the 'liquidity' and 'profitability' effects of incentives were considered important with liquidity being the more significant. Their results suggest, for example, that a 5 per cent increase in initial allowances would only raise investment by slightly more than 1 per cent in the first year with the 'profitability effect' operating. But in the second year, with both 'profitability' and 'liquidity' effects being felt, the rise in investment would be about 5 per cent. The effects of changes in investment allowances are greater. A 2.5 per cent change in investment allowances would change investment by almost 2 per cent in the first year and approximately 4 per cent by the third year. Although these results seem to produce a fairly clear picture of the effects of investment incentives, Agarwala and Goodson point out that their validity is limited by simplifying assumptions in the model and by the fact that possible multiplier effects of investment have not been taken into account. The use of a wider econometric model of the total economy was therefore advocated.

This positive finding was confirmed by Burman (1970) who also concluded that investment incentives could possibly play an important role in stimulating investment. Comparing the results of three investment functions estimated using quarterly data from 1956 to 1967 for manufacturing investment and from 1957 to 1968 for industrial and commercial companies' investment, he concluded that

> models in which the real cost of investment (actual investment reduced by present value of investment allowances and grants) was taken as the determinant variable imply that a given percentage rise in investment grants (or allowances) would increase investment in roughly the same proportion, because the real cost is about 50 per cent of the nominal cost. However, the fact that with other models the present value of allowances and grants did not show up as a significant financial variable suggests that there may be other explanations of this apparent effect.[7]

There is thus a clear note of caution.

A further study by Feldstein and Flemming (1971) similarly suggested that investment incentives have a significant effect on the level of investment. Feldstein and Flemming employed a generalised neo-classical model of investment behaviour to assess the effects of corporate taxation and investment allowances on the level of investment in manufacturing, construction, and distribution and other services using quarterly data from 1954 to 1967. Their results indicated that both the investment allowances and the tax incentive for increased retention of profits by firms had a substantial impact on investment. It was estimated, for example, that increases in depreciation allowances accounted for approximately 45 per cent of net capital accumulation in the period after 1954.

In contrast to the previous studies, Boatwright and Eaton (1972) were unable to show such positive effects when attempting to measure the impact of investment incentives on the level of fixed investment in plant and machinery in UK manufacturing industry using quarterly data over the period 1959 to 1970. In their model, they did not consider the allocation of funds in the firm but measured the effect of incentives through a change in the cost of capital. In evaluating the effect of investment incentives, three possible changes in incentives and taxation from the actual position since 1967 were examined – an increase in the cash grant by 5 per cent; no change in the level of allowances since 1967 but a reduction in corporation tax of 2.5 per cent; and a change to a new system of incentives with initial allowances of 35 per cent with corporation tax unchanged. Of these possibilities, the first two had relatively small effects, increasing investment by 1970 by 2.5 per cent and 0.5 per cent respectively. The third possibility would actually have decreased investment by 1970 by 4.5 per cent. Boatwright and Eaton qualified these results by saying that they should be regarded as provisional and that a wider corporate allocation of funds model was required. Nevertheless, their results suggest a much less significant role for investment incentives than that indicated by Agarwala and Goodson or Feldstein and Flemming.

Similarly, King (1972) concluded that the impact of investment incentives might not be as large as has been suggested by earlier studies. King examined the effects of taxation and investment incentives in a vintage investment model. This covered annual investment in plant and machinery by manufacturing industry over the period 1948 to 1968. In the analysis five series of the discounted value of investment incentives for plant and machinery were constructed using discount rates of 5 per cent, 10 per cent, $18\frac{1}{3}$ per cent and 25 per cent and 'first-year benefits only'. From these it was concluded that there was a substantial inducement to invest, the value of incentives in some cases amounting to around half the cost of the asset. However, the actual results derived from the model indicated that investment incentives had quite a weak impact on the level of investment. Although the effect will vary according to the level of discount rate used, at a rate of 18 1/3 per cent for example, the results implied that an increase in the rate of investment grants by 5 per cent would lead to an increase in investment in plant and machinery of 4.4 per cent. It was concluded by King that the response of investment to incentives was much smaller than that found in other studies. Feldstein and Flemming's estimate of the impact of tax allowances was about twice as large and that by Agarawala and Goodson about 25 per cent greater than the results implied in King's model.

To some extent the confusion of results was reduced by Sarantis (1979), who used an extended form of King's vintage model to examine the effect of incentives on manufacturing investment over the period 1954 to 1974. This showed quite a degree of responsiveness on the part of firms. The present value of all investment incentives for ten 2-digit manufacturing industries and total manufacturing industry was calculated using actual rates of return as a measure of the discount rate. Although there was a marked variation in a range of policy simulations, it was concluded that from 1954 to 1974 9.5 per cent of actual gross investment at 1970 prices could be attributed to investment incentives adopted in addition to normal depreciation allowances.

The results of the econometric studies have shown a relatively wide range in the effects of incentives on investment behaviour. A similar picture emerges from the results of studies carried out in the USA. There are several reasons why this should be the case which mainly relate to the underlying assumptions on which the econometric models are based and the data to which they have been applied. Each of the studies has differed somewhat in the form of investment function used and the efficacy of attempting to measure the effects of incentives in a single equation has been questioned. Different time periods and data have been used incorporating various rates and types of incentives. Strict comparison of the results is therefore difficult as the nature of the investment function and data used will ultimately influence the inferences that may be drawn from the studies. Although the studies provide a valuable insight into the possible effects of both tax incentives and direct grants, precise measurement of these effects remains indeterminate.

The survey and econometric studies of investment incentives in the UK have therefore not presented conclusive evidence of their effects on investment. Nevertheless, the evidence does suggest that incentives have had an impact on investment behaviour and both the 'liquidity' and 'profitability' effects have been seen as important. However, the studies have tended to concentrate upon effects which relate directly to the firm and aggregated investment. Little consideration has been given to the somewhat wider matter of the allocative effects and policy problems in stimulating investment through either the payment of direct grants to firms or through the fiscal structure.

## 5.5 INVESTMENT GRANTS AS AN ALTERNATIVE

Investment grants were introduced in 1966 not only with the intention of stimulating investment on a generalised basis, but also to provide a mechanism whereby incentives could be directed to particular sectors and regions of the economy. Tax investment incentives used since 1954 had been criticised on the grounds that they were unselective and non-specific. There were other difficulties in the application of incentives through the tax system. Because of the timing of corporation tax payments, firms could on average expect to experience a delay of some eighteen months between actual expenditure and the incidence of the incentive. Moreover, those firms not in a taxpaying position were not able to benefit immediately from the tax incentives so that their value diminished over time.

Although the system of grants was considered to be a solution to some of the criticisms levelled at tax investment incentives, it too gave rise to a number of problems in implementation. The system proved difficult to administer. Tax incentives were operated through an existing structure of corporate taxation and came under the jurisdiction of the Inland Revenue. Despite difficulty in determining whether some capital expenditures qualified for allowances, the system on the whole was comparatively straightforward. In contrast, the payment of grants involved the establishment of a separate Division within the Department of Industry and five regional offices.[8] The grant system was designed to be selective – assets of the service industries, for example, were excluded – and assets had to be used in a qualifying process. In addition, Development Areas received a higher rate of grant than the remainder of the economy. Each of these elements together with specific problems relating to areas such as hired assets required detailed processing and rendered the system complex.

In addition to administrative difficulties, perhaps the major criticism of the use of grants as an investment incentive was that it enabled both profitable and non-profitable firms to benefit which could 'result in uneconomic investment leading to waste of resources'.[9] Direct investment grants were therefore replaced by a return to tax investment incentives in the form of first-year capital allowances announced in October 1970.

## 5.6 ARE THE TAX INCENTIVES PASSED ON FROM LESSOR TO LESSEE?

As we have seen, one of the criticisms of tax incentives is that non-taxpaying firms are unable to take advantage of allowances immediately. It is important to stress that such firms have not necess-arily been unprofitable in the sense of being inefficient loss-makers, but rather many have simply lacked sufficient taxable profits against which allowances could be offset. Indeed, the increasing generosity of the corporate tax system during the 1970s meant that expanding firms with heavy capital investment could become rapidly tax ex-hausted. It has been argued that leasing allowed the transfer of much of the benefit of tax incentives from lessors primarily in the financial sector with taxable capacity to tax-exhausted firms in other sectors, particularly manufacturing. An important consideration in the con-text of the present discussion is the extent to which leasing has been effective in reallocating the benefits of incentives from lessor to lessee.

Although the empirical evidence is somewhat limited for the early 1970s, it would seem that in fact it has only been in relatively recent years that the majority of benefits has been passed to the lessee through the structuring of lease rentals. The evidence essentially takes two forms – studies of market structure and conditions, and analysis of specific leasing transactions. Study of the structure of the leasing market and its conditions will establish the degree of compe-tition amongst lessors and identify other market characteristics which can affect the distribution of tax advantage. *A priori*, it is to be expected that in the absence of competitive forces lessors will struc-ture lease rentals so as to retain a major proportion of tax benefit. Examining concentration ratios in the financial leasing industry in 1971, 1973, 1975, and 1977, Tomkins, Lowe and Morgan (1979) found the market to be 'fairly oligopolistic' and displayed 'a relatively high degree of concentration'. The dominant firms were the subsidi-aries of the four major clearing banks. The study also indicated that barriers to entry existed primarily in the form of taxable capacity, access to finance and availability of expertise and facilities for evalu-ating leasing terms. The present study has not found any specific evidence to indicate that the domination of the market by clearing bank subsidiaries has declined in the intervening period. Given such a market structure it is clearly possible that lessors could potentially utilise the position to gain a major share of the benefits of leasing. However there have been several new entrants to the industry, including overseas banks.

A further consideration in discussing the effectiveness of leasing in reallocating the benefits of tax investment incentives is the speed of adjustment of the market to changes in demand conditions. Since the emergence of a clear tax advantage, the supply of finance for leasing has been largely determined by the taxable capacity of lessors which is dependent upon the volume of leasing agreements written in the past and, in the case where lessors are subsidiaries, the amount of taxable profits of parent companies that can be used. Taxable capacity, therefore, cannot be varied significantly in the short run and so supply in the leasing market tends to be slow to react to rapid increases in demand. The demand for leasing facilities will be dependent upon the general level of demand for investment goods in the economy. It has also been strongly influenced by the growing incidence of firms in a non-taxpaying position in the non-financial sector. Devereux and Mayer (1984), using data for over 4000 principally large companies in manufacturing and distribution[10] have estimated, for example, that the percentage of companies with tax losses[11] rose from 14.8 per cent in 1971 to 54.7 per cent in 1981. If the supply of funds for leasing is unlikely to adjust rapidly to changing demand conditions then a situation of excess demand will result. Again, under these circumstances it is to be expected that much of the tax benefit of leasing will be retained by the lessor who is able to set the level of rentals accordingly.[12]

Both the structure of the market and operating conditions imply that leasing might not be a particularly efficient method of reallocating the tax benefits of investment incentives. There is some evidence to support this in the mid 1970s and beyond. Tomkins, Lowe and Morgan (1979, p. 47) have observed that by 1974–5, although a large number of lessors had become established in the market, conditions of rapidly growing demand meant that lessors margins were 'good' and competition was not 'severe'. The proportion of tax benefits retained by one lessor at this time was thought to be around 50 per cent. However, available evidence indicates that by the late 1970s much of the tax benefit was then being passed to the lessee. One possible source is to examine the profile of lease rentals over the period. Evidence of an increasing competitiveness in leasing rentals is by no means conclusive but it will indicate that lessors margins have decreased and this can be at least partly a product of transferring more of the tax benefit to the lessee. In articles published in its *Quarterly Bulletin*, the Bank Of England[13] has compared a range of effective leasing rates (i.e. the implicit interest cost of leases) for five year leases with money-market rates. If the position since the 1984 Budget, which rather distorted the market, is ignored, the data show that in the period of the second quarter of 1976 to the first quarter of

1984 leasing rates were quite substantially below money-market rates from the second half of 1979 onwards (for example, in mid 1980 there was approximately a difference of ten percentage points between the upper range of effective leasing rates and the Finance Houses Association base rate). Although the differential narrowed significantly by the second half of 1982 (for example, to two percentage points difference between the upper range of effective leasing rates and the Finance Houses Association base rate) and continued to narrow in 1983, reflecting changes in interest rate structures, by early 1984 the gap had begun to widen again. There are several reasons for the market becoming more competitive. On the supply side, taxable capacity has been influenced by the expansion of bank profits during periods of relatively high interest rates and the growth of rental incomes of lessors. An additional factor has been the entry of new lessors to the market and it is interesting to note that these have included quite a marked inflow of non-financial companies with taxable capacity. On the demand side, as potential lessees have gained knowledge of the advantages of leasing and the functioning of the market they have tended to seek the most competitive terms. Lease-brokers have played an important role in the process of disseminating information and negotiating competitive terms of their clients.

Although leasing rates provide an indication of growing competition and an increase in the amount of tax benefit being passed to the lessee, this source of evidence has been criticised by Edwards and Mayer (1983). They point out that the leasing rates on which the comparison by the Bank of England is based are published with the proviso that they only provide a general indication of a range of possible rates. Leasing rates in practice may vary considerably according to the circumstances of particular transactions. Edwards and Mayer therefore attempted to make a more accurate assessment of the distribution of tax savings between lessors and lessees by using data on 103 specific lease contracts. The results of an evaluation based on the assumption that the lessee is in a temporary non-taxpaying position are shown in Table 5.3.

Even though Edwards and Mayer fully accept that their exact figures are subject to some qualification and reservation, they conclude that their results are generally representative of the actual position during this period. On the basis of the analysis it was felt that since the end of the 1970s on average the majority of benefits from leasing accrued to the lessee.

*Table* 5.3   Effects on distribution of net present value of leases of lessee resuming paying tax – five year primary period leases

| Year of inception | No. of leases | Average % (assuming lessee permanently tax exhausted) to: | | Average % (assuming lessee tax exhausted for six years) to: | |
|---|---|---|---|---|---|
| | | Lessor | Lessee | Lessor | Lessee |
| 1977 | 9 | 34.4 | 65.6 | 45.3 | 54.7 |
| 1978 | 5 | 42.2 | 57.8 | 52.9 | 47.1 |
| 1979 | 8 | 19.3 | 80.7 | 25.7 | 74.3 |
| 1980 | 11 | 15.5 | 84.5 | 20.8 | 79.2 |
| 1981 | 17 | 17.2 | 82.8 | 23.7 | 76.3 |
| 1982 | 15 | 14.7 | 85.3 | 20.4 | 79.6 |
| Total | 65 | 16.87 | 83.13 | 23.18 | 76.82 |

*Source*:   Edwards and Mayer (1983) table 3.5, p. 44.

## 5.7   IMPLICATIONS

The evidence from the market and evaluation of specific leasing transactions show that increasing competition has led lessors to pass on more of the tax benefit to the lessee. An article on equipment leasing in the Bank of England *Quarterly Bulletin*, in 1980, concluded with the following observation:

> Leasing provides a good example of a competitive financial market. Notably, the profit margins obtained by lessors have declined as more lessors have entered the market or have been willing to commit more funds.
>
> The major benefit of leasing is that it provides a form of finance for industry that is cheaper than borrowing or instalment credit for a company that is not paying tax. With the reduction in lessors' margins that has occurred concurrently with the increase in interest rates accompanying inflation, the benefit to industry has increased.[14]

Prima facie evidence exists to support the central hypotheses that through the transfer of the benefits of capital allowances from lessors to non-taxpaying lessees, leasing has both increased the level of investment and changed its time profile by stimulating investment expenditure in periods of recession.

*Table* 5.4   Investment by manufacturing industry (pounds million at 1980 prices)

| Year | Own capital expenditure | Assets leased from the service industries | Total manufacturing investment |
|------|------|------|------|
| 1970 | 7990 | 160 | 8150 |
| 1971 | 7292 | 190 | 7482 |
| 1972 | 6344 | 160 | 6504 |
| 1973 | 6764 | 280 | 7044 |
| 1974 | 7397 | 320 | 7717 |
| 1975 | 6781 | 304 | 7085 |
| 1976 | 6437 | 317 | 6754 |
| 1977 | 6756 | 443 | 7199 |
| 1978 | 7203 | 662 | 7865 |
| 1979 | 7468 | 704 | 8172 |
| 1980 | 6445 | 830 | 7275 |
| 1981 | 4865 | 899 | 5764 |
| 1982 | 4458 | 1014 | 5472 |
| 1983 | 4373 | 797 | 5170 |

*Source*:   derived from 'Industry's Investment', *British Business* 8 June 1984, p. 173.

Table 5.4 shows the contribution of assets leased from the service industries to total manufacturing investment over the period 1970 to 1983.

As we have seen, the evidence from the Bank of England comparing leasing rates with other money-market rates shows that in general leasing rates were markedly below other money-market rates from mid 1979 but that the gap had narrowed significantly by the end of 1982. If the trend in leasing rates is compared with that of manufacturing investment over the same period, then it is immediately apparent that while 'own capital expenditure' has declined from 7468 million in 1979 to 4458 million in 1982 'assets leased from the service industries' has increased from 704 million to 1014 million. Leasing has expanded during a recessionary trend in manufacturing investment at a time when rates were particularly competitive and, as previously indicated, there was widespread tax exhaustion amongst firms. When leasing rates were closer to other money-market rates in 1983 leased assets fell back to 797 million. The prima facie evidence suggests that leasing may well have stimulated investment and acted in a counter-cyclical manner through lowering financial costs as a result of imbalance in the system of tax investment incentives.

In this chapter, we have seen that the evidence concerning the effects and effectiveness of investment incentives in general have left us with a rather unclear picture. However, there is considerable evidence to show that tax incentives have played a major role in leasing and to suggest that as an increasing share of the benefits of tax allowances were passed on by lessors to lessees, the level of leasing activity, and thereby its potential effect on investment, increased. To assess the precise magnitude of the relationship between leasing and investment we now turn to the evidence presented by econometric analysis.

# 6 Econometric Evidence

## 6.1 METHODOLOGY

It has been clear from the earlier chapters that survey evidence on the effect of leasing and other incentives is inconclusive but, on balance, indicates the existence of effects on the quantity and timing of investment. Econometric evidence on investment incentives is similarly mixed. However, it is unanimous in indicating some effect. The debate is over its size and consequently over its efficiency. None of the econometric evidence relates directly to leasing and as a consequence we need to undertake an analysis of our own.

The limited data on leasing permit a simple examination of our two major hypotheses: that leasing affects the level and timing of investment. By estimating a model to explain investment, the effect of leasing can be isolated by one of two means. Ideally leasing could be seen to have an effect on one or more of the determining variables in the model and hence its effect could be estimated directly by rerunning the model using the values that would have occurred without leasing. It was argued by several of the econometric modellers surveyed in the last chapter that leasing, for example, affected companies' cash flow and that cash flow in turn was a major determinant of investment. We could estimate a model of this two step relationship. An alternative approach is to see how much the structure of the investment equation changes with the advent of leasing. This second approach implies that leasing does not affect the determinants of investment but it affects the responsiveness of firms to the determinants. These are both testable hypotheses.

The first approach is the more attractive as it does not require strong assumptions for its validity. There are two widely used forms of explanation for investment.[1] One of them is the augmented accelerator model, through which investment depends upon lagged values of output and various other variables reflecting the firm's ability to pay. The second emphasises the role of the relative prices of inputs to the productive process – largely labour and capital – and derives investment demand through an explicit process of optimisation on the part of the firm.[2] These are usually thought of as neo-classical models. Their important feature is that they incorporate into the equation the cost of capital. Since one of the main reasons adduced for using leasing is that it reduces the cost of capital, there is therefore an incentive to use this type of model. The basic difficulty is to estimate how much leasing would have reduced the cost of capital.

The degree of cost change depends upon the tax position of the firm. If the firm is not tax exhausted then the cost advantage of leasing is likely to be limited. The attractiveness of leasing will then depend upon the other factors listed in Chapter 1. Only some of these will have a measurable effect on the cost of capital, such as cash flow advantages. This presents great difficulties. It is possible to derive estimates of the cost of capital for lessees and purchasers. However, by definition in an aggregate model tax exhausted firms and those with taxable capacity are taken together. While weighting may be possible it is very difficult to incorporate this as it is in many ways a jointly determined variable depending upon the decision whether to lease or purchase as the latter contributes to tax exhaustion.

The most promising approach may be to examine models such as that of Bean (1979) which, although incorporating a flexible accelerator, have as their additional variables factors relating to cost. In this case they are the rate of interest and the real cost of capital. (Bean also has a variable showing the proportion of firms facing capacity constraints. Here the argument is simply that firms with spare capacity are less likely to invest.)

The problem facing us in this study is whether to estimate our own investment equations and then include them in a macroeconomic model or to take existing equations and try to calculate how they are affected by leasing. The attraction of estimating our own equation is that it can be explicitly specified to include variables directly related to leasing. The drawback is the inserting of new equations in existing models which itself presents difficulties. In the first place, it will alter the properties of the entire system as macroeconomic models are in large measure simultaneous. Thus before using the revised model it would be necessary to test the properties of the new system. This is not an impossible task but certainly a substantial one.

The second difficulty concerns the variables on the right-hand side of the equation. Several such as output, interest rates or cash flow will be clearly endogenous. However, unless they are specified in conformity with the rest of the model they will not be properly determined within it. Further equations will therefore have to be respecified and re-estimated, again not impossible but a much more complicated route.

We therefore chose the simpler solution of using an existing model. Here the problem is that the specification may not be ideal for our purpose, but we felt this was the lesser of the two difficulties.


## 6.2  CHOICE OF MODEL

The choice of appropriate model for incorporation in our study is a difficult one. The model must have separate equations for manufacturing investment, public sector investment and investment by the rest of the private sector as a minimum disaggregation. Fortunately, with the foundation of the ESRC Macroeconomic Modelling Bureau at the University of Warwick, most of the main models of the UK economy are readily available with a simulation package, so access is not a binding criterion. The choice essentially lay between the Treasury model (HMT), the London Business School Model (LBS) and the National Institute model (NIESR).

Other models of the economy do exist but were quickly rejected for practical and theoretical reasons. The disaggregated Cambridge Growth Project model with its forty sector breakdown of industry is more complex than necessary and has a weaker macroeconomic structure than some of the others. The Liverpool model unfortunately poses some difficulties for simulation which would constrain the outcome in a way inappropriate for our purposes. The City University Business School (CUBS) model stresses supply factors and the Oxford Economic Forcasting model (OEF), although suitable in structure, is only available commercially and not through the ESRC Macroeconomic Modelling Bureau.

It is, of course, mistaken to talk about these models as a single entity. They tend to evolve rapidly over time. The versions available to us were not identical to those being used by the three organisations mentioned and are certainly not the same as those currently in use.

It was decided to use the National Institute model (version 7, November 1984) as this is particularly well suited to our needs as it not only has the appropriate disaggregation, separating out manufacturing and services investment, but identifies leasing quite explicitly in its formulation. It assumes that leasing by the manufacturing industry is bahaviourally the same as investment by manufacturing industry, implicitly assuming in effect that leasing is just a different method financing the investment. Leasing to the manufacturing industry is therefore subtracted from investment by the distribution and services sector and added to that by manufacturing industry before any estimation takes place.

## 6.3  LEASING AND INVESTMENT BY MANUFACTURING INDUSTRY

The investment equation for manufacturing industry used in the National Institute Model 7 is:

$$QDKMFA = 16.8 + 1.26QDKMFA_{-1} - 0.326QDKMFA_{-2}$$
$$\quad\quad\quad (0.3)\ \ (12.4) \quad\quad\quad\quad (3.1)$$

$$+\ 2.59\triangle(UTIL\ OMF)_{-1} + 2.37\triangle(UTIL\ OMF)_{-2}$$
$$\quad (2.9) \quad\quad\quad\quad\quad\quad (2.5)$$

$$+\ 277.4\triangle CF + 211.6CF_{-3} + 148.7DG - 267.0DG_{-1}$$
$$\quad (2.4) \quad\quad\quad (2.5) \quad\quad (2.9) \quad\quad (5.1)$$

$$+\ 201.3DG_{-2}$$
$$\quad (3.6)$$

$OLS$, $R^2 = 0.94$, $SEE = 48.5$, $LM(8) = 12.0$ (1966(1)–1983(2))

where:

$QDKMFA$ is investment in manufacturing including leasing (and excluding metals);

$UTIL$ is a capacity utilisation variable (CBI Survey);

$OMF$ is a manufacturing output index;

$CF$ is a cash flow term defined as the real level of non-North Sea company sector post-tax profits net of stock appreciation;

$DG$ is a dummy variable which is unity 1968(4) and zero in all other periods to take into account a change in the rate of investment grants.

The equation contains terms relating to the cash flow of the firm. Leasing is expected to affect the cash flow of the firm and hence there is likely to be some interaction between these terms. However, the measuring of 'cash flow' in these two cases may not be identical. In the sense of the equation it is the ex-post result, whereas it is rather more of an operating condition in terms of the benefit conveyed by leasing as described in the surveys.

The National Institute equation has a further problem in that the sum of the lag coefficients on investment is near unity. This problem would result in there being no equilibrium level for investment if the coefficients were exactly unity. Over some time periods, 1966(1) to 1976(4), for example, this lack of equilibrium occurs.

The procedure followed was twofold. In the first place the National Institute equation was re-estimated using their data, which they kindly supplied on the assumption that leasing caused a structural shift in the equation. As we have seen, the equation is of the form:

$$QDKMFA = b_0 + b_1 QDKMFA_{-1} + b_2 QDKMFA_{-2}$$
$$+ b_3 (UTIL \times OMF)_{-1} + b_4 (UTIL \times OMF)_{-2}$$
$$+ b_5 CF + b_6 CF_{-3} + b_7 DG + b_8 DG_{-1}$$
$$+ b_9 DG_{-2} + e$$

If we simplify this to

$$QDKMFA = \mathbf{Z}\mathbf{b} + e$$

where

$$\mathbf{Z} = \begin{bmatrix} 1 \\ QDKMFA_{-1} \\ QDKMFA_{-2} \\ \triangle(UTIL \times OMF)_{-1} \\ \triangle(UTIL \times OMF)_{-2} \\ \triangle CF \\ CF_{-3} \end{bmatrix} \quad \mathbf{b} = \begin{bmatrix} b_0 \\ b_1 \\ b_2 \\ b_3 \\ b_4 \\ b_5 \\ b_6 \end{bmatrix}$$

then we can estimate the structural change by the equation

$$QDKMFA = \mathbf{Z}\mathbf{b} + \mathbf{Z}\mathbf{D}\mathbf{c} + e$$

where $\mathbf{D}$ is an identity matrix in the period after leasing started to become important and a null matrix beforehand. The terms in $DG$ are unaffected and included as before as they have their effect in 1968–9 before leasing began its rapid expansion.

The vector $\mathbf{c}$ shows the effect of the structural change. Before the rise of leasing $\mathbf{Z}$ affects investment by $\mathbf{b}$, after the rise the effect is (**b** + **c**). However, we cannot distinguish the degree to which the structural change was due to leasing from the degree to which it was due to other factors which happened to occur at the same time. Furthermore, the representation of the structural change as a simple switch is an exaggeration. We therefore experimented both by varying the timing of the change and its duration.

This method also has the disadvantage that if there is any variable that also becomes important in explaining investment in the presence of leasing but which is omitted from the equation, then all the remaining coefficients will be biased except in the unlikely event that the omitted variable is orthogonal to the others. The second approach to estimation of the effect of leasing on the economy was to estimate investment functions for the period before leasing became important and then run a dynamic forecast over the remaining years. A dynamic forecast is one where the forecast values from the previous periods are fed back into the equation as inputs for further years, as opposed to a static forecast which uses the actual values of the variable in the past. Thus the static forecast will tend to bring the equation back on track while the dynamic one can diverge progressively as one error builds on another. This is because if, as in this case, investment in previous periods is included in the equation in the dynamic forecast, the equation's own forecasts of investment in the earlier equation are included. Whereas in the static case the actual value is included. If the equation is wrong and, say, forecasts investment too low, this will then feed back into the equation in the subsequent period and, since the coefficient is positive, make the next forecast even lower still, perhaps causing an explosive downward error. The effect of leasing is then estimated as the difference between the actual value of leasing and that forecast. This again has the disadvantage that changes due to that cause are caught up in this estimate. These extra effects could be positive or negative so we cannot even suggest that the estimate represents some sort of upper limit.

It is clear from Figure 6.1 that investment is a highly cyclical variable. There have been three complete cycles since 1967 with peaks in 1969, 1973 and 1979 and it appears that a fourth peak has been reached in 1985, although it is too soon to say if this will be another straightforward cycle. Leasing, over the same period, rose slowly up to 1976 and much more rapidly since then reaching a sharp peak in 1985(1) (see Figure 6.2). The 1985(1) peak, largely influenced by the 1984 Finance Act is excluded from estimation. Cash

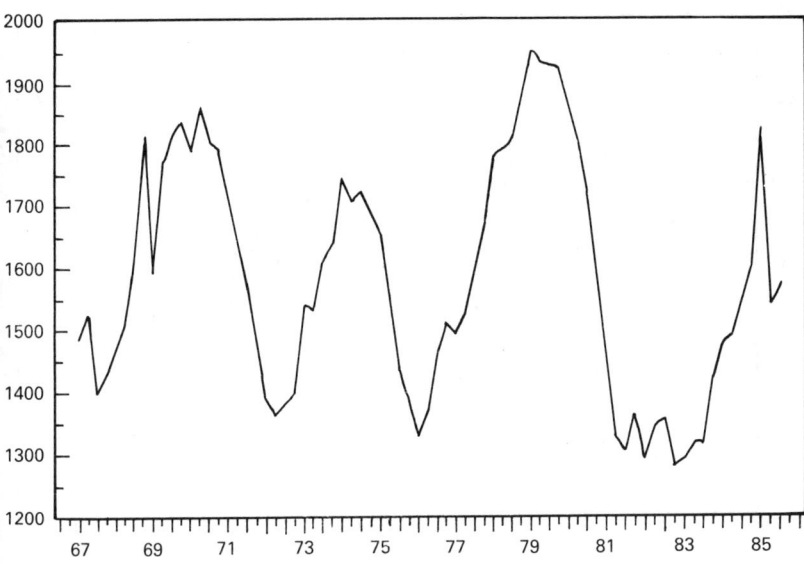

*Figure* 6.1   Level of investment including leasing (1967 Q1 to 1985 Q3)

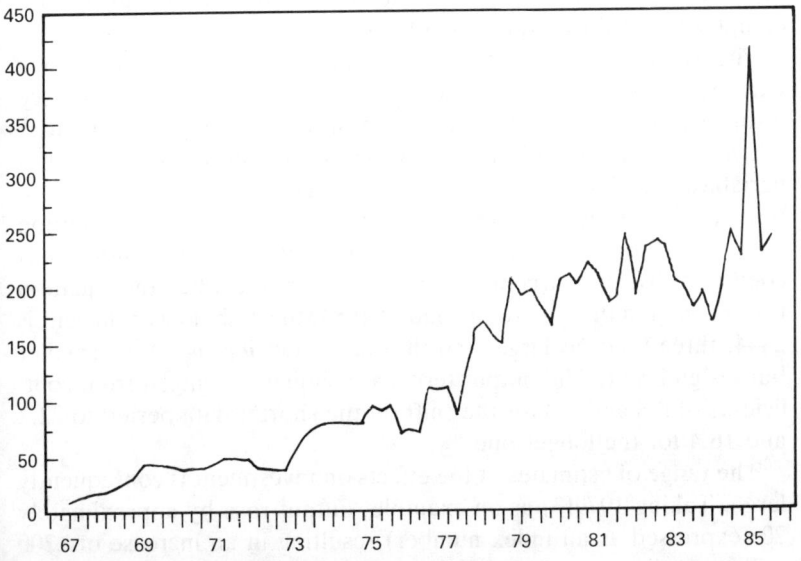

*Figure* 6.2   Level of leasing (1967 Q1 to 1985 Q3)

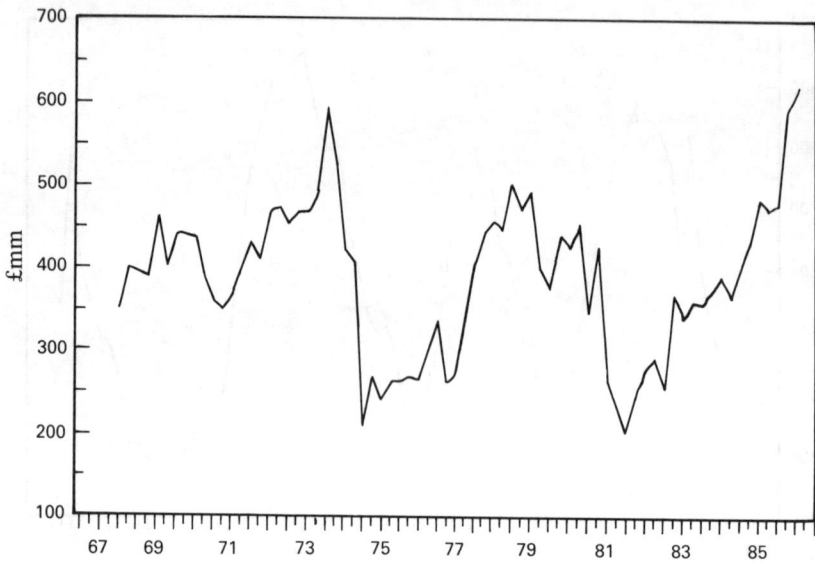

*Figure* 6.3    Level of cash flow (1967 Q1 to 1985 Q3)

flow, shown in Figure 6.3, also has a cyclical pattern, but a more complex set of fluctuations than for investment.

First of all, estimating the National Institute equation with leasing excluded over the periods (1966(1)–1980(4) and 1966(1)–1984(4) (see Table 6.1 [3] it is clear that there is a major increase in investment after the first quarter of 1977 when leasing became important. The shift variables are clear although only marginally significant. The equations obviously fluctuate considerably. While the long-run solution has a cash flow coefficient of 785 in the shorter data set, with a shift coefficient twice as large for the post 1976 period, when the equation is re-estimated through to the end of 1984, the cash flow coefficient is 2444, three times as large, and the shift coefficient is a little smaller but insignificant. The output terms are similarly changed from coefficients of 8.8 and 9.8 for the shift on the shorter data period to 22.2 and 16.4 for the longer one.

The range of estimates of the effects on investment is consequently large. Taking 1979(3) as an example, output rose by approximately 20 (expressed as an index number) resulting in an increase of £200 million in investment for the quarter on the basis of the shorter period (9.8 × 20) and £330 million on the basis of the longer period

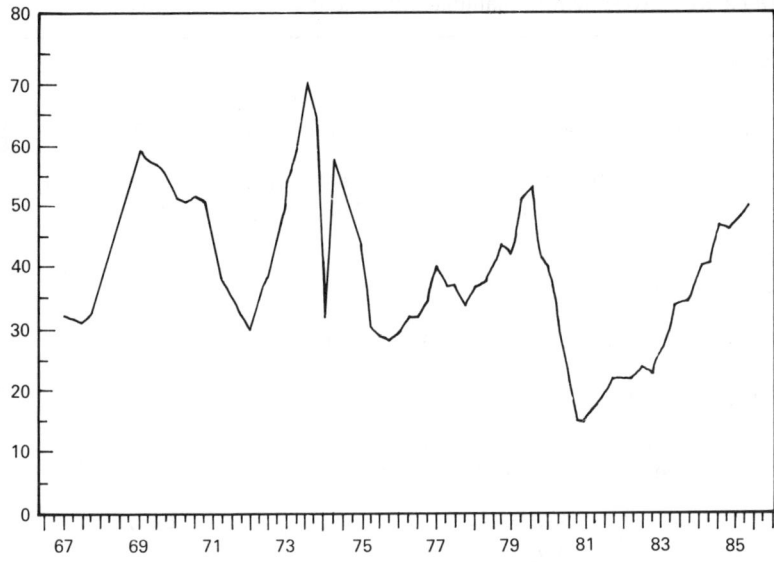

*Figure* 6.4   Level of UTIL × OMF (capacity utilisation × output) (1967 Q1
to 1985 Q3)

(16.4 × 20). The size of leasing itself was £200 million per quarter at
that time, so if all this change was due to leasing then leasing resulted
in an increase in investment between 2 and 2 2/3 times its own value.
The cash flow term has a further effect of some £550 million per
quarter. It does not seem plausible to attribute such a large effect to
the impact of leasing.

If we look at the estimates with leasing included (Table 6.2) we can
see that there is no evidence of a structural shift in the output effect,
but the cash flow effect is a coefficient of about 2000 in both regres-
sions. This would give an effect of around £700 million per quarter at
the mean. Since actual leasing was £200 million this implies an extra
effect of some £500 million per quarter, increasing investment
through the cash flow term. This might imply that leasing had eased
cash flow constraints.

In either event, these equations imply a big increase in investment
other than for leasing. It is not clear whether this can be attributed to
leasing or other unknown factors.

If the second method of dynamic forecasting is used then the
results are corroborated. Using the equation excluding leasing, set

*Table* 6.1 Investment in manufacturing industry excluding leasing

---

*1966(1)–1980(4)*

$$I_t = 214 + 0.73I_{t-1} + 0.56I_{t-2} - 0.49I_{t-3} + 258\triangle CF_t + 157CF_{t-3} + 1.76\triangle_3 UY_{t-1}$$
$$\quad (2.7) \quad (6.8) \qquad (4.0) \qquad (4.2) \qquad (2.2) \qquad (1.7) \qquad (2.8)$$

$$-0.62(I \times D)_{t-2} + 0.51(I \times D)_{t-3} + 4.62(CF \times D)_{t-3} + 3.04\triangle_3(UY \times D)_t$$
$$\quad (1.9) \qquad\qquad (1.6) \qquad\qquad (2.0) \qquad\qquad (1.8)$$

$SE = 44.75, dw = 2.1$
with a long-run solution

$$I = 785CF + 1500(CF \times D) + 8.8\triangle_3 UY + 9.8\triangle_3(UY \times D)$$

*1966(1)–1984(4)*

$$I = 36 + 0.83I_{t-1} + 0.44I_{t-2} - 0.36I_{t-3} + 229\triangle CF_t + 220CF_{t-3} + 2.0\triangle_3 UY_{t-1}$$
$$\quad (0.7) \quad (8.5) \qquad (3.3) \qquad (3.2) \qquad (2.1) \qquad (2.4) \qquad (2.8)$$

$$- 0.40(I \times D)_{t-2} + 0.35(I \times D)_{t-3} + 171(CF \times D)_{t-3} + 2.3\triangle_3(UY \times D)_{t-1}$$
$$\quad (1.9) \qquad\qquad (1.7) \qquad\qquad (1.0) \qquad\qquad (1.7)$$

$SE = 45.6, dw = 1.8$
with a long-run solution:

$$I = 2444CF + 1221(CF \times D) + 22.2\triangle_3 UY + 16.4\triangle_3(UY \times D)$$

---

*Note*: Using the original NIESR model terms $QDKMFA = I_t$, $UTIL = U$ and $OMF = Y$

out in Table 6.3, we observe that investment is underforecast during the period of growth up to 1979 but overforecast in the period of decline (Figure 6.5). In the lease inclusive case the whole forecast is shifted downwards because of the direct effect of leasing on investment (Figure 6.6).

The reason this apparently perverse effect occurs in the downturn is because investment depends upon the change in output not on its level. Hence with the substantial slump in output occurring after 1979 (see Figure 6.4) investment is forecast to fall less before the structural change occurred. This has some awkward implications for our hypothesis that leasing affects the timing and levels of investment.

The conclusion from the initial estimate remains. It is likely that leasing contributed to a rise in investment larger than its own size.

*Table* 6.2    Investment in manufacturing industry including leasing

---

*1966(1)–1980(1)*

$$IL_t = 272 + 0.77IL_{t-1} + 0.49IL_{t-2} - 0.46IL_{t-3} + 263\triangle CF_t + 91CF_{t-3}$$
$$\quad\;\;(3.4)\qquad\quad (3.5)\qquad\quad (4.1)\qquad\quad (2.1)\qquad\quad (1.0)$$

$$+ 2.2\triangle_3 UY_{t-1} - 0.86(IL\times D)_{t-2} + 0.70\,(IL\times D)_{t-3} + 568(CF\times D)_{t-3}$$
$$\quad (2.5)\qquad\qquad\;\; (2.2)\qquad\qquad\qquad (2.4)$$

$SE = 43.93,\; dw = 1.99$
with a long-run solution:

$$IL = 455CF + 1893(CF\times D) + 11.2\triangle_3 UY$$

*1966(1)–1984(4)*

$$IL = 99 + 0.90IL_{t-1} + 0.34IL_{t-2} - 0.33IL_{t-3} + 247\triangle CF_t + 125CF_{t-3} + 2.9\triangle_3 UY$$
$$\;(1.8)\;(9.0)\qquad\quad (2.5)\qquad\quad (2.9)\qquad\quad (2.9)\qquad\quad (2.1)\qquad\quad (1.5)\qquad\quad (2.9)$$

$$-0.36(IL\times D)_{t-2} + 0.28(IL\times D)_{t-3} + 356(CF\times D)_{t-3}$$
$$\quad (1.8)\qquad\qquad\quad (1.5)\qquad\qquad\qquad (2.0)$$

with long-run solution:

$$IL = 1389CF + 2094(CF\times D) + 32\triangle_3 UY$$

---

*Table* 6.3    Manufacturing investment equations 1966(1)–1976(4)

---

*Excluding leasing*

$$I_t = 247 + 0.80I_{t-2} + 0.47I_{t-2} - 0.45I_{t-3} + 2.23\triangle_3 UY_{t-1} + 256\triangle CF_t + 99CF_{t-3}$$
$$\;(2.4)\quad (7.0)\qquad\;\; (3.1)\qquad\;\; (3.6)\qquad\quad (3.0)\qquad\qquad\;\; (1.8)\qquad\quad (1.0)$$

$R^2 = 0.90,\; SE = 46.2,\; dw = 1.9$

*Including leasing IL*

$$IL_t = 208 + 0.77IL_{t-1} + 0.52IL_{t-2} - 0.47IL_{t-3} + 1.78\triangle UY_{t-1} + 256\triangle CF_t + 163CF_{t-3}$$
$$\;(2.3)\quad (6.9)\qquad\quad (3.7)\qquad\quad (3.8)\qquad\quad (2.5)\qquad\qquad\; (1.9)\qquad\quad (1.7)$$

$R^2 = 0.91,\; SE = 44.6\; dw = 2.0$

---

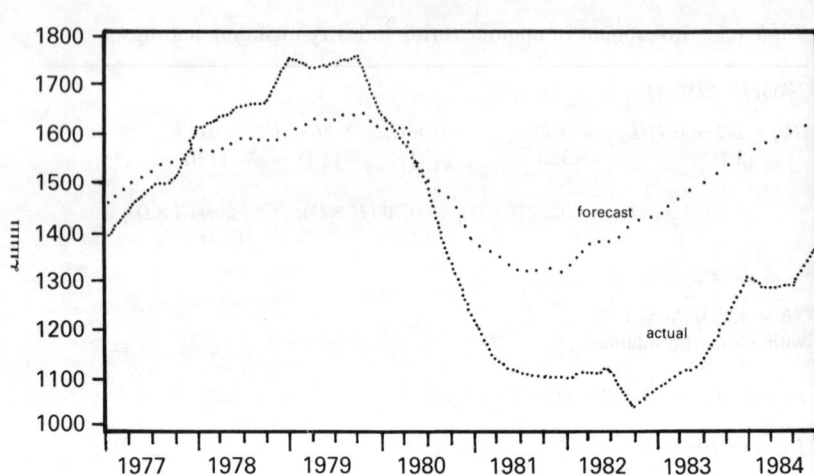

*Figure* 6.5    Investment excluding leasing (I): dynamic forecast 1977(1)–
               1984(4)

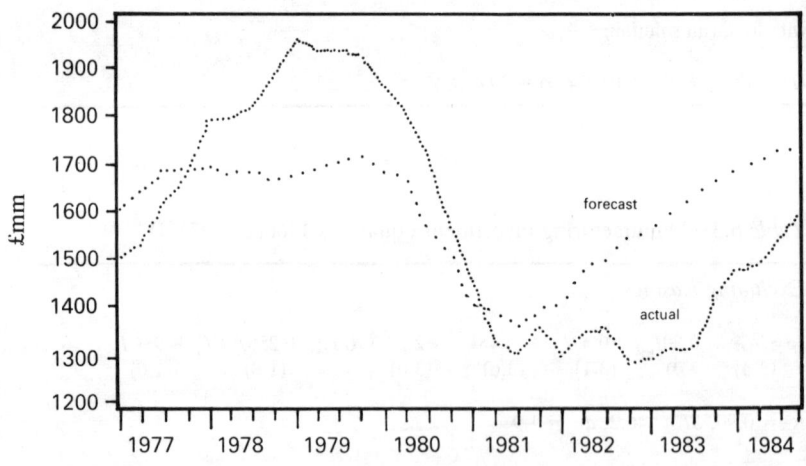

*Figure* 6.6    Investment including leasing(II): dynamic forecast 1977(1)–
               1984(4)

## 6.4 LEASING AND INVESTMENT BY SERVICE INDUSTRIES

Since the use of leasing transfers investment expenditures from the category of manufacturing to services there is a worry that it may in fact reduce the level of investment by the service industries for their own use. However, this does not appear to be the case. The equation explaining investment by the services industries excluding leasing is hardly changed over the period 1977–85. A second hypothesis would be that leasing actually increased investment by the service industries. The evidence suggests that there is weak support for such an effect.

Using the form of investment function in the National Institute model 7 as in the case of manufacturing the original equation is:

$$IS = 20.0 + 0.631KS_{-1} - 0.623KS_{-2} + 91.0DH - 41.6DH_{-2}$$
$$(0.6) \quad (8.0) \qquad\quad (7.8) \qquad\qquad (2.8) \qquad (1.3)$$

$$+ \ \Sigma a_i \Delta C_{-i}$$

| i | $a$ | $t$-statistic |
|---|---|---|
| 1 | 0.0175 | 1.0 |
| 2 | 0.0301 | 1.7 |
| 3 | 0.0283 | 1.7 |
| 4 | 0.0414 | 2.5 |
| 5 | 0.0393 | 2.2 |
| 6 | 0.0811 | 4.5 |
| 7 | 0.0308 | 1.7 |

$$\Sigma a_i = 0.269$$

$OLS$, $R^2 = 0.98$, $SEE = 55.8$, $LM(8) = 11.9$ (1967(2)–1983(2)).

where:

*IS* is investment in distribution and business services excluding leasing
*KS* is the capital stock in distribution and business services
*C* is consumers' expenditure
(all in constant 1980 prices)
*DH* is a dummy variable with the value unity between 1969(3) and 1973(1) (zero elsewhere) to take account of the stimulus given to hotel building by the Development of Tourism Act (1969).

Reparameterising this equation in a more parsimonious fashion (this is the jargon expression for re-estimating the equation in a simplified form) gives:

$$IS = 348 + 0.41KS_{-1} - 0.40KS_{-2} + 0.04\triangle_5 C_{t-1}$$
$$\quad (7.9)\ (4.4) \qquad (4.3) \qquad (2.9)$$

$$+ 0.09\triangle C_{t-6} + \quad 0.09\triangle C_{t-7}\ (+ \text{ dummy variables})$$
$$(4.0) \qquad\quad (4.1)$$

$$SEE = 44.6,\ DW = 1.9\ (1967(2)\text{--}1976(4))$$

when run over the period before the rise in leasing.

This equation has the long-run form:

$$IS = 580 + 0.64\triangle \bar{C}$$

where $\bar{C}$ is the mean value of $C$.

The equation was then re-estimated for the periods 1967(2) to 1980(4) and 1985(3). These all gave very similar results. Taking 1967(2)–1980(4) as an example, using dummy variables to take account of changes in the parameters since 1976(4) adds the further terms:

$$+ 0.02\triangle_5(C \times D)_{t-1} + 0.04\triangle(C \times D)_{t-6} + 0.04\triangle(C \times D)_{t-7}$$
$$(0.8) \qquad\qquad\quad (0.9) \qquad\qquad\quad (0.8)$$

$$- 574D - 0.57(KS \times D)_{t-1} + \quad 0.59(KS \times D)_{t-2}$$
$$(2.4) \quad (2.6) \qquad\qquad\quad (2.6)$$

$$SEE = 47.8,\ DW = 2.2$$

Only the capital stock and constant terms show significant changes in parameters. The new long-run solution in the period when leasing became important is:

$$IS = -193 + 0.81\triangle \bar{C}.$$

The change in the constant is the stronger effect thus suggesting lower investment.

However, if the dummy variable on the constant term is omitted:

$$IS = 327 + 0.41KS_{-1} - 0.40KS_{-2} + 0.043\triangle_5 C_{-1} + 0.091\triangle C_{-2}$$
$$(6.7) \ (3.9) \qquad (3.8) \qquad (2.7) \qquad (3.6)$$

$$+ \ 0.093\triangle C_{-3} - 0.52(KS \times D)_{-1} + 0.02\triangle_5(C \times D)_{-1}$$
$$(3.6) \qquad (2.2) \qquad (1.1)$$

$$+ \ 0.08(C \times D)_{-6} + 0.08(C \times D)_{-7}$$
$$(1.9) \qquad (1.0)$$

$$\Sigma\triangle C \text{ coefficients} = 0.399$$

$$\Sigma\triangle(C \times D) \text{ coefficients} = 0.262$$

$$\text{together} = 0.661.$$

It is thus clear that the coefficient on consumers' expenditure in the long run is virtually identical. In the period of leasing, though, the effect feeds through onto investment rather more quickly.

If we take the second approach, which is to use the pre-leasing equation to forecast the outcome after leasing became important, we find that positive residuals build up quickly even in the static forecast mode (i.e. using actual values of the lagged dependent variable):

| year | residual £m | (%) |
|------|------|------|
| 1977 | 20 | 1.2 |
| 1978 | 62 | 3.6 |
| 1979 | 104 | 5.2 |
| 1980 | 109 | 5.2 |

In the dynamic forecast mode, allowing the model itself to generate the lagged values of the dependent variable, the divergence rapidly becomes massive. However, with a standard error of £44.6m even the 1980 figure is only a little over two standard deviations from the mean value – well inside the forecast error bounds at the 95 per cent level. There is thus only weak evidence of a positive effect of leasing on non-leasing investment in services and the appropriate conclusion is probably that there is no impact.

Thus from the point of view of investment by the services industries leasing is an addition, it neither adds nor subtracts from what previous behaviour suggests would have happened. Therefore, since leasing led to an increase in investment in manufacturing industry, that increase, seen across the whole of private sector investment, can be taken as the measure of how much investment increased as a result of leasing. There was no offsetting movement in the services sector and some limited indication that it too may have increased.

## 6.5   THE EFFECTS OF LEASING ON THE ECONOMY AS A WHOLE

In view of the range of possible effects of leasing on investment we have run a very simple simulation with the National Institute model (version 7) by assuming that half leasing represents an increase in investment over what it would have been otherwise. The model was therefore rerun over the period 1975(1) to 1985(4) with a residual of minus half the value of leasing imposed on the manufacturing invest-ment equation. As is clear from Table 6.4, not surprisingly, the main impact is to deflate the economy. Gross Domestic Product (GDP) is 2 1/2 per cent lower by the end of the period and unemployment higher by around 300 000. This is thus not a minor change. If similar results were to be observed as a consequence of the 1984 Finance Act, the cost of the reduction in tax allowances would, at current long-run growth rates, be equivalent to one year's growth in ten. However, in that case leasing is maintained but at less attractive terms.

It is clear immediately from these figures that any counter-cyclical effect from leasing is dominated by the rate of rise of leasing itself. Since there is a multiplicative element involved as the reduction in investment feeds through the economic system, it is not possible merely to relate the effect on GDP from the ending of leasing with the cycle in economic growth on a direct period by period basis. Thus, while leasing may have been relatively higher in a recession, much of its effect has been generated by the 'knock on' impact of falls in investment in previous years.

While the simulation thus appears to support the hypothesis that leasing has aided economic growth and unemployment quite substan-tially, it provides only limited evidence to support the assertion that leasing has a beneficial effect (in the macroeconomic sense) on the timing of investment.

Within the individual sectors of the economy the path of the effect

*Table* 6.4   Effect of removal of leasing on the UK economy 1975(1)–1985(4)
(% change from base)

| GDP | Consumers' expenditure | Invest- ment | Exports | Imports | CPI | Real incomes | Unem- ployment '000 |
|---|---|---|---|---|---|---|---|
| 1975(4) – 0.2 | 0.0 | – 1.9 | – 0.2 | – 0.9 | – 0.2 | – 0.0 | 9 |
| 1976(4) – 0.4 | 0.0 | – 3.2 | – 0.7 | – 1.7 | – 0.7 | – 0.1 | 29 |
| 1977(4) – 0.6 | 0.0 | – 4.8 | – 1.1 | – 2.6 | – 1.5 | – 0.2 | 52 |
| 1978(4) – 0.9 | 0.0 | – 8.0 | – 1.5 | – 3.8 | – 2.7 | – 0.3 | 80 |
| 1979(4) – 1.2 | 0.0 | –10.2 | – 1.9 | – 4.6 | – 4.1 | – 0.4 | 121 |
| 1980(4) – 1.4 | 0.1 | –12.2 | – 2.4 | – 5.5 | – 6.0 | – 0.4 | 153 |
| 1981(4) – 1.7 | 0.1 | –14.5 | – 2.8 | – 6.2 | – 8.2 | – 0.4 | 189 |
| 1982(4) – 1.9 | 0.3 | –15.6 | – 3.2 | – 6.5 | –10.8 | 0.0 | 227 |
| 1983(4) – 2.1 | 0.6 | –15.5 | – 3.9 | – 6.3 | –13.9 | 0.4 | 260 |
| 1984(4) – 2.2 | 0.8 | –16.1 | – 4.5 | – 6.3 | –17.0 | – 0.8 | 289 |
| 1985(4) – 2.4 | 1.1 | –17.2 | – 4.4 | – 6.1 | –20.1 | 1.4 | 317 |

Effect falls mainly on investment although the price level is some 20 per cent lower after eleven years.

is quite complex. Because prices are kept lower rather more than earnings are, real incomes rise towards the end of the period. This effect and the direct price effect lead to an increase in consumers' expenditure in the second half of the period. The favourable price movement lowers imports relative to exports but as consumer demand picks up imports also begin to rise relative to their values in the base solution.

These movements may be telling us more about the specific workings of the National Institute model in such a long simulation than about the detailed impact of leasing. The important point to bear in mind is that the effects tend to be limited since in the long run most models tend to an underlying growth path. Hence, in this form of simulation the outcome may be a path below that of the base solution but not diverging further after a while.

If the coefficients in the equation are changed, as suggested in

Section 6.3 above, then the effect may come through rather more strongly onto the rate of growth. As investment is an essential input to the process of increasing future output, the growth rate will be lower in the future if leasing would have increased its share of investment. If, however, it would have reached a maximum level then growth would peak in the long run and the absence of leasing would have led to a once and for all loss of output during the period when leasing's contribution would have risen. Since the experience in other countries (see Chapter 7) suggests that leasing tends to settle to a relatively stable proportion of investment as the process of market penetration comes to an end, then leasing could continue to affect not just the level of activity in the economy but its rate of growth as well.

Our figures are inconclusive as leasing had not reached maximum market penetration by 1985 and hence the simulation could not show what the mature market position would result in. All we can say is that, over the period 1975–85, if leasing had not existed the UK economy would have grown more slowly.

Clearly, one could undertake further simulations which would seek to examine what would have happened if the extra tax revenue earned in the absence of leasing had been spent, or if taxes had been reduced by an equivalent amount. Just cutting leasing might not be viewed as a neutral simulation in policy terms. The government might have reacted by making an offsetting change to keep their borrowing requirement at the same level which would have stimulated the economy by a different route. It is well known that the route of stimulus, whether by direct or indirect tax cut or capital or current expenditure increase, has a considerable effect on the overall outcome.[4] It would therefore be necessary to simulate a variety of hypotheses to form a clear picture. Since this is all hypothetical we have not done so but since the increase in government revenue is only likely to be about half the value of the fall in investment (at the prevailing tax rates), the offsetting stimulus would need to be similarly effective if the net effect were not to be negative.

## 6.6  ECONOMETRIC SUPPORT FOR THE PRINCIPAL HYPOTHESES

Taking the econometric evidence as a whole there is clear support for a substantial effect from the rise of leasing on the level of investment in the UK in the period since 1974. This effect on investment had consequences for the growth of the economy as a whole which would have been about 1/4 per cent lower in the absence of leasing, as indicated by the National Institute model. Such a small sounding change is in fact a very major contribution to easing the problems of the economy when it is realised that it represents avoiding unemployment of some 300 000 people by the end of a decade (i.e. 10 per cent of the total unemployed).

Leasing has played a major role in the growth of the economy. However, this is not to say that alternative financial instruments would not have been introduced which would have had an equal or even greater impact.

The role of leasing in speeding recovery from economic recessions, although borne out by the evidence, does not appear to be strong despite the clear motivation for it from tax exhaustion. The main reason for this appears to be that leasing was on such a strong growth path over the period that it had not hit demand constraints by the first peak of activity in 1979, and hence was still growing as the recession ensued despite the overall fall in investment. The cyclical element would only be readily observable when leasing followed more of a stable path among the various sources of finance. The 1984 Finance Act means that this possibility will still not occur for some time.

Thus, we must conclude on the basis of the survey and econometric evidence that leasing did indeed enable a clear increase in investment by tax exhausted manufacturing companies in the period after 1979, hence contributing to economic growth. The cyclical element would only have become clear in a further recession as it was not until 1982–3 that the rise in leasing faltered whereas the trough of the recession was in the first half of 1981.

# 7 The Experience in Other Countries

As an integral part of the testing of the central hypotheses concerning the tax-based effects of leasing on investment, we have examined patterns of leasing in other countries to determine the extent to which the expansion of leasing in the UK has been specific to domestic institutional arrangements and conditions. The extent to which leasing has increased overseas where similar tax incentives do not exist may give an indication of the size of tax-based leasing in the UK. Furthermore, the existence and success of different leasing practices overseas can act as a basis for assessing what might be adopted or be successful in the UK.

There are several inherent difficulties in making direct comparisons between leasing activity in different countries which will ultimately limit, to some extent, the validity of conclusions based on such evidence.[1] Official statistics vary widely in availability from country to country and in some cases simply do not exist. Furthermore, for those that are available there are considerable divergences in statistical definitions and coverage; methods of collection and sources of data; and the manner in which leasing statistics are treated in national accounts. Definitions of leasing range from 'finance leasing' (in some countries this includes a purchase option whereas in others it is similar to UK usage of the term) through separate definitions of finance and operating leasing to relatively wide definitions involving no clear distinction between finance leasing and operating leasing. There is also variation in precisely what is included in leasing statistics (e.g. whether lessors in the non-financial sector are taken into account or how assets leased abroad are treated). Data are collected from lessors only in some countries whilst in others information is gathered from both lessors and lessees. Thus, apart from definitional problems of comparison which are largely rooted in the different legal and accounting structures of individual countries, there are substantive differences in the amount of data available extending from basic expenditure series to very comprehensive data including detailed breakdown of the structure of the leasing industry (i.e. number of enterprises, employment, etc.), expenditure on leased assets and analysis of lessees. The limitations of official statistics therefore make it difficult to derive strictly meaningful comparative data on the contribution of leasing to investment in individual countries.

Data have consequently been obtained from a number of additional sources, including correspondence with national leasing organisations and individual lessors, supplemented by personal interviews in France, West Germany and the Netherlands and 'Leaseurope' statistics.

Accepting that there are serious limitations of comparability, on the basis of available information, it has been possible to make general observations which are of relevance to the primary research objective. The general pattern which has emerged so far from the cross-national comparisons is that the contribution of leasing to capital formation and counter-cyclical tendencies have generally been more significant in countries where tax advantage has been present.

We have already demonstrated the importance of tax advantage in the growth of leasing in the UK. However, it is the case that leasing has also grown in countries where tax environments have not been so favourable. Table 7.1 shows the development of new leasing business for Leaseurope members over the period 1979 to 1982. It is evident from these statistics that significant amounts of leasing have been

*Table* 7.1　Leaseurope members' new business 1979–82 (in ECU)

|  | 1979 | 1980 | 1981 | 1982 |
|---|---|---|---|---|
| Austria | 137 | 181 | 176 | 198 |
| Belgium | 154 | 170 | 149 | 222 |
| Denmark | 63 | 67 | 86 | 287 |
| Finland | 67 | 136 | 284 | 333 |
| France | 2964 | 3477 | 3511 | 3739 |
| Germany | 1074 | 1173 | 1512 | 1858 |
| Ireland | 38 | 15 | 39 | 49 |
| Italy | 727 | 1233 | 1657 | 1778 |
| Luxembourg | 5 | 6 | 8 | 15 |
| Netherlands | 456 | 524 | 532 | 525 |
| Norway | 98 | 125 | 262 | 464 |
| Spain | 151 | 210 | 309 | 381 |
| Sweden | 246 | 310 | 622 | 592 |
| Switzerland | 187 | 268 | 304 | 381 |
| UK | 3258 | 4265 | 4835 | 4861 |

*Source*:　Leaseurope.

undertaken in countries such as France, West Germany and the Netherlands where tax considerations have not been particularly important.

Although we have previously identified inherent difficulties in comparing leasing activity between countries and its role in relation to investment, Clark[2] has compiled data on the penetration of leasing in capital formation for OECD countries over the period 1978–82 which are shown in Table 7.2. Clearly some caution should be exercised in interpreting these data for there are likely to be variations in the conceptual base and consequent coverage relating to individual countries. Nevertheless, the data are useful in providing a generalised indication of the respective positions of the various countries. The information in Table 7.2 indicates that, in countries such as the UK or USA where tax considerations have been important in the development of leasing, a significant degree of penetration has been achieved. A particularly interesting example of the effect of tax investment incentives has also been provided by the experience of the leasing market in Sweden. In correspondence with a Swedish lessor, it was indicated that an Investment Tax Credit of 20 per cent for investments during the period 1980–1 had substantially increased leasing activity since a large number of companies were not in a taxpaying position during that period. Furthermore, the same lessor also commented that profitable companies in Sweden had bought lease portfolios to reduce corporate taxes by utilising depreciation allowances and the effect of this had been the lowering of the cost of leasing and its increased use. This is reflected in the data relating to Sweden in Table 7.2. It is also interesting that a withdrawal of Investment Tax Credits in Sweden in January 1984 has resulted in a 50 per cent reduction in new investment in leasing.[3] Again, in Table 7.2 there is evidence to suggest that leasing activity has been significant in countries such as France where it has achieved marked penetration in capital formation in an environment where tax advantage has not played a major role in the growth of leasing.


## 7.1 FRANCE

Modern leasing was introduced into France in the early 1960s. Unlike the growth of leasing in the UK, the development of leasing in France has not been predominantly influenced by tax advantage. Depreciation allowances have tended not to be of significance and provision

Table 7.2  Penetration of leasing in capital formation 1978–82

|  | 1978 % | 1979 % | 1980 % | 1981 % | 1982 % |
|---|---|---|---|---|---|
| **North America** |  |  |  |  |  |
| Canada | 4.4 | 6.3 | 5.6 | 4.7 | 3.3 |
| United States | 15.6 | 17.0 | 21.9 | 25.6 | 27.9 |
| Average | 14.7 | 16.1 | 20.4 | 23.6 | 25.5 |
| **Europe** |  |  |  |  |  |
| Austria | 1.9 | 2.6 | 3.0 | 2.8 | 2.8 |
| Belgium | 2.6 | 3.4 | 3.3 | 3.0 | 4.6 |
| Denmark | 1.3 | 1.9 | 2.0 | 2.6 | 8.3 |
| Finland | 1.4 | 2.4 | 3.7 | 6.6 | 7.2 |
| France | 6.8 | 7.9 | 7.9 | 7.3 | 8.5 |
| Germany | 2.0 | 2.2 | 2.2 | 2.8 | 3.0 |
| Ireland | 0.5 | 0.5 | 0.6 | 1.6 | 2.0 |
| Italy | 4.7 | 5.2 | 5.3 | 6.2 | 6.8 |
| Luxembourg | 0.5 | 3.1 | 2.2 | 2.5 | 5.1 |
| Netherlands | 4.7 | 5.1 | 5.9 | 6.2 | 5.1 |
| Norway | 2.8 | 2.7 | 3.3 | 5.6 | 9.8 |
| Spain | 2.5 | 3.6 | 2.2 | 3.2 | 4.5 |
| Sweden | 3.0 | 4.1 | 4.5 | 8.5 | 9.0 |
| Switzerland | 2.0 | 3.7 | 4.5 | 5.1 | 4.9 |
| United Kingdom | 8.0 | 10.0 | 11.6 | 13.3 | 13.0 |
| Average | 4.3 | 5.2 | 5.6 | 6.3 | 6.9 |
| Japan | 4.8 | 5.8 | 6.2 | 7.0 | 8.3 |
| **ANZ** |  |  |  |  |  |
| Australia | 26.4 | 30.2 | 25.0 | 22.2 | 23.1 |
| New Zealand | 3.6 | 4.9 | 3.0 | 14.2 | 20.4 |
| Average | 24.4 | 27.8 | 23.7 | 21.5 | 22.8 |
| Overall penetration | 9.2 | 10.5 | 12.3 | 14.1 | 15.0 |

Notes:

1. The penetration of leasing figures represent leasing investments (i.e. annual expenditure by leasing companies on plant and equipment for leasing) as a percentage of total capital formation.

2. Figures for leasing investments are those published by the American Association of Equipment Lessors, Statistics Canada, Leaseurope and the Japan Leasing Association (adjusted to calendar years) and are the authors' estimates for Australia and New Zealand.
3. Figures for capital formation are derived from the transport equipment, machinery and other equipment categories of Gross Fixed Capital Formation in OECD National Accounts.
4. All currency conversions to US dollars have been at average 1982 exchange rates.
5. Constant price figure adjustments have been based on OECD rates of inflation.

*Source*: Compiled by T.M. Clark and published in the *World Leasing Yearbook* (Hawkins Publishers, 1985) p. 19.

for 'group relief' has not been generally available. Consequently, there is little inherent tax benefit to the lessor or lessee from leasing. Leasing has therefore grown for other reasons. The fact that it enables a company to acquire assets without large capital outlay has been regarded as an important contributing factor to growth, since many companies in the French economy have (in the past decade in particular) increased their level of gearing and yet have also not had sufficient total funding to replace aging capital equipment. Equally, the relative ease with which a lease can be set up (weeks as opposed to months), the absence of large front-end fees, and its overall flexibility when compared to other sources of finance have been important. The fixed nature of the lease contract has also been an attraction in a country where in the past monetary policy has been punctuated by periods of credit restriction.

Both finance and operating leasing exist, although the market tends to be dominated by the former. The leasing market in France is highly regulated and this has affected both the practice of leasing and the overall market structure. The law of 2 July 1966 (as amended 28 September 1967) rendered leasing subject to earlier laws relating to the regulation of banking, and legally defined the concept of finance leasing (*crédit-bail*). Article 1 defines *crédit-bail* as

transactions involving the hiring of capital, goods or tooling equipment which are destined for professional use and are purchased in view of such hiring companies which remain the owners thereof, when such transactions however they may be termed, give to the lessee the option of purchasing all or part of the equipment leased at an agreed price which takes into account at least in part the payments made as rentals.

*Crédit-bail* is divided into two separate categories – *crédit-bail mobilier* (movable assets) and *crédit-bail immobilier* (fixed assets). *Crédit-bail mobilier* is generally used to describe equipment leasing whereas *crédit-bail immobilier* relates mainly to real-estate leasing.

From the definition of *crédit-bail* it is immediately apparent that finance leasing in France differs fundamentally from that in the UK, because in France there is an option to purchase the asset at a fixed price (normally around 4–6 per cent of the initial cost) at the end of the primary period. If the option is not exercised then the lessee may continue leasing for a further period at reduced rentals or return the asset to the lessor. The structure of *crédit-bail* therefore has characteristics of both finance and hire and lies between finance leasing and hire purchase as practised in the UK. In addition, it is worth noting that the term 'professional use' in the legal definition excludes consumer goods and leasing to individuals or assets for professional use without a purchase option (which is considered operating leasing). Such leases, which fall outside the scope of *crédit-bail*, are generally termed 'renting' and are less widely used although in recent years the amount of operating leasing undertaken in France has increased.

Moreover, as well as defining *crédit-bail*, the 1966 law relating to leasing has also regulated the type of organisation which may offer this form of finance. *Crédit-bail* is regarded as an industrial credit facility in the same way as bank term lending and may therefore only be transacted by a registered financial institution (*etablissement financier*) or bank (*banque*) if deposit-taking. Registration involves a complex array of regulations governed by the laws relating to banking and similar activities concerning, for example, reserves, capital structure, organisation and management and regular reporting to the central bank authorities.

The regulation of lessors in France and the lack of substantial tax advantage has been reflected in the structure of the market which has been dominated by wholly owned subsidiaries of banks and by independent leasing companies. In the absence of significant tax benefit and the presence of laws which regard leasing essentially as a financial facility, a strong non-financial lessor sector has not developed. Similarly, as a result of the complexity of establishing a finance leasing company in France there have tended to be few foreign-owned leasing companies. There are also several small leasing companies operating, sometimes on a local basis, but, like foreign owned lessors, these do not form a large part of the market. However, the position in the French leasing market is likely to change somewhat. A

*Table* 7.3  Growth of *crédit-bail* in France, 1973–83 (investment in millions of francs)

|  |  | *Annual growth %* |
| --- | --- | --- |
| 1973 | 10381 | |
| 1974 | 10714 | + 3.2 |
| 1975 | 10050 | − 6.2 |
| 1976 | 12461 | +24.0 |
| 1977 | 12983 | + 4.2 |
| 1978 | 13636 | + 5.0 |
| 1979 | 14351 | + 5.2 |
| 1980 | 16730 | +16.6 |
| 1981 | 18312 | + 9.5 |
| 1982 | 22666 | +23.7 |
| 1983 | 25192 | +11.1 |

*Source*:  Institut National de la Statistique et des Etudes Economiques, *Enquête Annuelle d'Enterprise, Crédit-Bail*, 1983, table 15, p. 42.

new Banking Act of 24 January 1984 made it mandatory for all leasing companies to register as credit institutions before May 1985. The new legislation will bring all leasing activity under regulation.

Official statistics for leasing have in the past related only to finance leasing but will now expand to take into account these changes. At the time of this report, the available data are still for finance leasing (*crédit-bail*). Table 7.3 shows the growth of total *crédit-bail* over the period 1973 to 1983.

The relationship of leasing to overall investment is somewhat difficult to distinguish in the case of France. When interviewed, a representative of the French leasing organisation, Association Français-aise des Sociétés Financiers – ASF, held that leasing had increased the level of investment although he was unable to suggest what proportion of leasing formed additional investment and what consti-tuted substitution for other forms of finance. Analysis of available data suggests that leasing has tended to vary somewhat as a propor-tion of investment expenditure in France. Table 7.4, for example, shows equipment leasing and investment in machinery and equip-ment over the period 1970 to 1983. Equipment leasing has been used most extensively in the service and industrial sectors but has not developed significantly in construction and agriculture. Within the industrial sector lessees in the intermediate and capital goods indus-tries have accounted for the largest part of the market, whilst in the service sector distributive trades, transport and telecommunications

*Table* 7.4   Equipment leasing (*crédit-bail mobilier*) and investment in machinery and equipment 1970–83 (current prices, in Ffr. bn)

|  | Total investment in machinery and equipment | % of total capital equipment New investments in assets for leasing | % of total capital equipment |
|---|---|---|---|
| 1970 | 70.9 | 2.7 | 3.8 |
| 1971 | 79.9 | 3.6 | 4.5 |
| 1972 | 88.8 | 5.5 | 6.2 |
| 1973 | 101.9 | 7.2 | 7.1 |
| 1974 | 117.5 | 7.5 | 6.4 |
| 1975 | 122.9 | 7.4 | 6.0 |
| 1976 | 149.3 | 10.1 | 6.7 |
| 1977 | 164.8 | 10.6 | 6.4 |
| 1978 | 183.0 | 11.1 | 6.1 |
| 1979 | 207.7 | 11.6 | 5.6 |
| 1980 | 247.9 | 13.1 | 5.3 |
| 1981 | 271.2 | 13.8 | 5.1 |
| 1982 | 306.6 | 18.2 | 5.9 |
| 1983 | 324.7 | 19.7 | 6.1 |

*Sources*:   OECD National Accounts and INSÉE.

and market services have been important areas. Data processing and electrical equipment, vehicles, office and industrial machinery have been the major types of asset leased.

It can be seen that in 1970 equipment leasing formed some 3.8 per cent of gross fixed capital formation in machinery and equipment. By 1983 the figure stood at 6.1 per cent although it had reached a peak of 7.1 per cent in 1973 and fluctuated in the intervening period. With the exception of 1975, when equipment leasing actually declined, the long-term trend in current prices has been upward. However, if growth in real terms is considered this pattern no longer holds. Table 7.5 shows the data at constant 1980 prices.

This indicates that after sharp increases in the early 1970s equipment leasing declined in real terms in 1974 and 1975. Substantial growth was experienced in 1976 followed by a downturn until 1982 and also a slight fall in 1983. Clearly this does not indicate steady growth and when compared to movements in investment does not suggest that leasing has had a counter-cyclical influence. When investment in machinery and equipment fell in real terms in 1975

*Table* 7.5   Equipment leasing (crédit-bail mobilier) and investment in machinery and equipment 1970–83 (1980 prices, in Ffr. bn)

|  | Total investment in machinery and equipment | New Investments in assets for equipment leasing |
|---|---|---|
| 1970 | 178.1 | 6.8 |
| 1971 | 190.2 | 8.6 |
| 1972 | 199.1 | 12.3 |
| 1973 | 213.2 | 15.1 |
| 1974 | 216.0 | 13.8 |
| 1975 | 202.1 | 12.2 |
| 1976 | 223.9 | 15.1 |
| 1977 | 226.1 | 14.5 |
| 1978 | 230.2 | 14.0 |
| 1979 | 235.7 | 13.2 |
| 1980 | 247.9 | 13.1 |
| 1981 | 239.1 | 12.2 |
| 1982 | 241.8 | 14.3 |
| 1983 | 233.6 | 14.2 |

*Sources*:   OECD National Accounts and INSÉE (converted to constant prices using INSÉE deflator).

(largely as a result of the oil shock) equipment leasing also declined. This was also the case in 1981 and 1983. Thus although it is considered that leasing may have had an effect on the quantity of investment in France, there is little evidence to suggest that it has actually encouraged investment in periods of recession. The major difference in pattern from the UK has been the lack of any period of rapid growth over the last decade. Leasing appears to have obtained a share of the market by 1972–3 and merely maintained it since then. This might perhaps be regarded as a saturation level.

## 7.2   WEST GERMANY

Available evidence also indicates that the growth of leasing in West Germany has been achieved largely without the degree of tax advantage that has existed in the UK. Leasing developed in West Germany in the early 1960s. Data on the total value of new investments in leased assets collected by survey by the Ifo-Institute (an independent research body) demonstrate rapid growth since the early 1970s, especially in the latter part of that decade. New investments in leased

*Table* 7.6  Dietz survey of reasons for leasing results relating to West Germany

| Reason | Percentage of firms |
| --- | --- |
| Liquidity | |
|   100% finance | 74 |
|   Credit links remain open | 66 |
|   Capital freed | 65 |
| Protection against obsolescence | 55 |
| Fixed costs | 72 |
| Tax advantages | 63 |
| Parallel between costs and return | 63 |
| Cheaper than other credit | 49 |
| Balance sheet neutrality | 46 |
| Effect as regard inflation | 32 |

assets (including real-estate) grew from some Dm. 4330 million in 1972 to Dm. 18 170 in 1984.[4] This growth has been achieved as a result of a number of essentially non-tax-based reasons.

A survey of lessees concerning reasons for leasing conducted by Dietz (1977) showed that 100 per cent finance, fixed costs and preservation of existing lines of credit were considered particularly important. The results relating to West Germany of a question asking which factors were thought very important in the leasing decision are shown in Table 7.6.

An interview with the West German leasing organisation, Bundes-verband Deutscher Leasing Gesellschaften eV (BDL), indicated that off-balance sheet characteristics of leasing in West Germany had been important because of the implications for gearing in relation to the financial position of firms as profits have been squeezed. The question of balance sheet disclosure is determined by which party to the lease is deemed to have either economic or beneficial ownership of the asset. As legal owner of the asset the lessor is generally considered to be the beneficial owner, providing that the risk of any loss or potential gain in the value remains with the lessor. If the lessor is held to be beneficial owner then the asset is capitalised in his balance sheet. If the lessee is beneficial owner then the agreement is held to be that of hire purchase. Other factors such as the avoidance of large capital outlay and cash flow advantage were identified. It was also thought that the fact that leased assets could be treated as current rather than capital expenditure, thereby lowering the level of investment decision-making within organisations, had been influential in the growth of leasing.

Leasing in West Germany includes both equipment leasing and real-estate leasing. Equipment lessors include small private companies, non-financial sector companies as well as subsidiaries of domestic banks. Subsidiaries of foreign leasing companies are also present. It is interesting to note that subsidiaries of domestic banks do not have a dominant position in the market, and in fact leasing has tended to be regarded in West Germany as being essentially outside the mainstream financial world. It is not subject to the same regulation as banking.

A broad range of equipment is leased, extending from office equipment to blast furnaces. However, office equipment and computers have formed a major part of the market with vehicles and plant and machinery also accounting for significant proportions of assets leased. In terms of lessees, the manufacturing sector has been most important.

Recent Ifo-Institute estimates show that in 1984 leasing, including real-estate, formed some 7.1 per cent of capital investment (excluding private housing). Its growth in relation to investment is shown in Table 7.7.

Although leasing has expanded (with the exception of 1984) year on year, there is little evidence of a strong counter-cyclical influence upon investment. It was thought by the BDL that it was unlikely that leasing has had much impact on the quantity of total investment but it

*Table* 7.7   Growth of leasing and capital investment in West Germany (in Dm. million)

|  | *Total capital investment (excl. private housing)* | *Total value of new investments in leased assets at cost* | *% of total capital investment* |
|---|---|---|---|
| 1976 | 164500 | 6270 | 3.8 |
| 1977 | 176420 | 7690 | 4.4 |
| 1978 | 194300 | 9780 | 5.0 |
| 1979 | 220300 | 11770 | 5.3 |
| 1980 | 242080 | 13170 | 5.4 |
| 1981 | 243270 | 16450 | 6.8 |
| 1982 | 237420 | 17250 | 7.3 |
| 1983 | 246440 | 18670 | 7.6 |
| 1984 | 256100 | 18170 | 7.1 |

*Source*:   Ifo-Institute

was felt that, through its advantages, leasing had a positive effect on the timing of investment expenditures. In this case leasing was continuing to increase its share of total investment but only at a relatively slow rate.

## 7.3   THE NETHERLANDS

An interview was also conducted with a representative of the national leasing organisation in the Netherlands, Nederlandse Vereniging Van Leasemaatschappijen. Although detailed statistics from the industry have not been provided relating to the growth of leasing in the Netherlands and no official statistics are currently available, it was made clear that there had been a steady development since its introduction in 1963 and that this had not been aided on the whole by tax-related factors.[5] An important consideration here is the division of leases in the Netherlands into finance and operating leases principally on the basis of economic rather than legal ownership. Finance leasing accounts for a major share of leasing activity. Central to this distinction is the question of which party bears the economic risk – in the case of the finance lease it is the lessee whilst the lessor does so under an operating lease. Thus through the use of finance leasing the lessee acts basically as owner and therefore enters the lease in his accounts. The lessee is also considered owner for fiscal purposes if he bears the risks of changes in the value of an asset and so can claim depreciation allowances or investment incentives directly. Similar considerations of economic ownership also apply, for example, in Austria and Belgium. It is interesting to note that there have been recent moves in the Netherlands towards placing economic risk more with the lessor under operating leasing, with the lessor able to claim investment incentives and pass the benefit to the lessee in the form of lower rental payments.

Leasing facilities in the Netherlands are made available through commercial banks, finance companies and leasing companies. The latter includes manufacturers which use leasing as an aid to 'sell' their products. Finance companies and leasing companies may be subsidiaries of banks and other financial institutions.

Assets leased in the Netherlands range widely but in general assets which are specialised and/or which do not have substantial residual value tend to be avoided. Because of the possibility of *bodembeslag* (i.e. the fiscal authorities can seize movable assets in the case of default on tax payments) lessors generally favour leasing to firms with a strong financial base. This applies principally to finance leasing and not normally to operating leasing where, as we have seen, it is deemed that the lessor has full economic ownership.

Among the reasons cited for leasing in the Netherlands were: the lowering of decision-making levels within organisations; the increasing use as a sales-aid; difficulty in obtaining medium-term fixed interest rate finance; past difficulties with fluctuating rates of interest; and the fact that the contract can be repudiated earlier and with less consequence compared to ownership.

Leasing accounts for about 6 per cent of investment in capital goods but it was thought to have little effect on the total level of investment as firms could raise finance from other sources.

The interviews conducted and information obtained on leasing in France, West Germany and the Netherlands have shown that the growth in the use of leasing has not been limited to economies where tax benefit has played an important role. However, it is noticeable that growth in the use of leasing and its consequent impact upon the economy has tended to be greater in countries where tax-based leasing has been significant.

## 7.4 THE UNITED STATES

In addition to the growth of leasing in the UK, tax considerations have also been very influential in the USA. Precise analysis of the position in the USA has proved to be somewhat difficult because there would appear to be relatively few conclusive statistics on leasing. The collection of official data tends to be decentralised with a number of separate agencies obtaining information in different sectors and at different levels. For example, the US Department of Commerce Bureau of the Census collects data from the manufacturing sector whilst the Bureau of Economic Analysis collects data from the financial, insurance and real-estate sectors. Data are obtained at the level of the operating unit or establishment and at the level of the firm or business unit. However, the types of statistics on leasing activity varies from sector to sector. It is therefore difficult to determine precisely the development of leasing from such sources. The American Association of Equipment Lessors (AAEL) has data derived from annual surveys of its members carried out by Deloitte, Haskins and Sells. Response rates have tended to vary from year to year. Recent figures indicate that the total cost of new equipment added in 1983 was $8.7 billion rising from $8.4 billion in 1982.

However, despite difficulty in obtaining suitable data, there have been recent changes in fiscal legislation affecting leasing which provide some evidence of the importance of tax advantage in the USA. The mechanism through which tax advantage is gained by leasing in America is similar to that in the UK. If a firm purchases an asset, normally an investment tax credit (ITC) and accelerated depreciation are available. The ITC allows the firm to deduct a proportion of the original cost of the asset from its tax liability. Although there are provisions to carry forward both incentives, if the firm does not have sufficient taxable profits, their value will decline over time if not utilised. A taxpaying lessor can capture the advantage of these tax incentives and can transfer some of the benefit to the non-taxpaying firm as lessee through reduced rentals.

Lessors have therefore been able to allow non-taxpaying firms to obtain at least in part the benefits of the ITC and accelerated depreciation but this has applied only to 'true' leases. However, these leases have not always been attractive to firms because they include a number of restrictions. For example, to be deemed a 'true' lease the fiscal authorities require that an agreement does not contain a 'bargain fixed price purchase option'. Other requirements include the limitation of the lease to 80 per cent of the useful life of the asset, the prohibition of the lessee to finance any part of the purchase price of the asset and the leasing of 'limited use' property. Partly in order to relax such restrictions, and in an attempt to stimulate investment, 'safe harbour leasing regulations were introduced in the 1981 Economic Recovery Tax Act (ERTA). This allowed all firms investing in new assets to gain from tax incentives. The Act introduced the Accelerated Cost Recovery System (ACRS) which enabled firms to depreciate assets over a shorter period than previously allowed. ERTA permitted non-taxpaying firms to acquire assets through firms ('nominal lessors') with tax liability. These 'nominal lessors' leased back the asset to the non-taxpaying firm whilst benefiting from the investment tax credit and accelerated depreciation. In this way the non-taxpaying firm was able to acquire assets at a considerably reduced cost. The requirements of a qualifying lease were ammended to include 'bargain fixed price purchase options'. In addition, lessees could lend the lessor up to 90 per cent of the purchase price of an asset, and leases of more than 80 per cent of the useful life of an asset and of 'limited use' property were included. A substantial amount of assets were leased as a result of ERTA. However, it was felt that large taxpaying firms, particularly financial institutions, were the main beneficiaries and that the loss of revenue to the Treasury Department was not justified. The Tax Equity and Fiscal Responsibility Act of 1982 (TEFRA) was therefore designed and introduced effectively to remove most of the 'safe harbour' regulations by the end of 1983, but the increase in depreciation allowances through ACRS remained. Although the effects of ERTA were relatively short-lived, they do provide an illustration of the significance of tax advantage and market reaction to changes in tax legislation relating to leasing.

Further evidence of the importance of tax advantage in US leasing has been indicated by the response of the leasing industry to recent proposals to reform the tax system (i.e. 'Treasury I', 'Treasury II' and the Ways And Means Committee Staff Proposals). In addition to other provisions, these have advocated the removal of the investment tax credit, revision of the accelerated cost recovery system of depreciation, a cut in the rate of corporation tax and a minimum corporation tax. The American Association of Equipment Lessors has campaigned strongly against such reform. In a statement to the House Committee on Ways and Means, the AAEL said:

> Over its 30 year history, the equipment leasing industry has grown to become the largest external source of capital in America for investment in equipment. Our association represents over 900 leasing companies. In 1984, over $74 bn worth of capital equipment was put to work through leasing. Through financial expertise and asset risk management, equipment lessors help to put productive equipment to work for business and industry – large and small. As you can see, these companies have a direct concern in our country's economic growth, particularly in investment in productive assets such as equipment.[6]

The statement also indicated that leasing 'can utilize the tax incentives of equipment ownership to reduce capital costs when a user company cannot' and that 'the immediate impact of most of the tax reform proposals will be to increase the costs of equipment to American business, industry and agriculture by on average amounts of between 9 per cent and 11 per cent'.

The AAEL have characterised the effects of implementing tax reform proposals under the following headings:

— less equipment acquisition,
— less demand for tax-oriented products,
— decrease in the attractiveness of providing leasing by lessors,
— increase in attractiveness of alternative investment opportunities [to lessors],
— decrease in players in the market-place.[7]

Although the US leasing market would undoubtedly survive and adjust to tax reform, the implication of the reduction of tax incentives would be a decline in investment which would be reflected in the rate of growth of the US economy.


## 7.5   IMPLICATIONS

Because of the rather limited nature of some of the data collected from other countries and the problems of making direct comparisons between very different legal and fiscal environments, any conclusions based on such information should be regarded with some caution. However, a number of clear points of relevance to the basic research objective have emerged.

Leasing has grown both in countries where tax considerations have been favourable or essentially neutral. This suggests that growth is not totally dependent upon tax advantage and there are other reasons for leasing. As we have seen, many of the non-tax reasons are related to cash flow advantages, the provision of an additional source of finance and balance sheet disclosure requirements. It would appear that leasing has been particularly used in situations where firms' financial resources are stretched but additional or replacement equipment is required. This may arise from specific factors such as investment in cost-saving capital following the oil crises in the 1970s or from general conditions such as the need to invest in new plant and machinery when faced with an aging stock. Leasing has enabled firms to acquire the use of assets without severe impact on cash flow and when finance from other sources is limited. Non-disclosure in the balance sheet is also of significance as a consequence of its effects upon the apparent gearing structure of the firm and the manner in which its capital structure is viewed by other providers of finance.

However, although leasing has grown for reasons other than tax benefit, it would appear that its development has been stronger where such advantage has existed. Tax advantage has affected both the supply of funds for leasing and the demand for leasing facilities and this has been reflected in the cost of finance to the firm. The availability of tax advantage is clearly dependent upon the structure of fiscal regulations relating to tax investment incentives. In countries such as the UK where the lessor is considered owner for fiscal purposes, firms in a non-taxpaying position are able to gain access to incentives through leasing in the form of reduced rentals. In countries such as the Netherlands, under a finance lease the lessee is considered fiscal owner where he bears the risks and changes in asset value. The lessee thus depreciates the asset in his balance sheet and is able to claim investment incentives directly.

The data have also indicated that leasing has tended to have a more marked impact upon investment where tax advantage has been present. Prima facie evidence has been provided in Clark's figures in Table 7.2. His estimates of the penetration of leasing in capital formation show that in 1982, for example, in the USA leasing formed some 27.9 per cent of capital formation and 13 per cent in the UK – both countries where there has been a tax advantage in leasing – compared to 4.9 per cent in Switzerland and 5.1 per cent in the Netherlands where tax considerations have not been largely influential. Our evidence suggests that the effect of leasing on investment is likely to have been greater in terms of volume and to have exerted counter-cyclical tendencies in countries where leasing has facilited the transfer of the benefits of tax investment inventives from lessor to lessee.

# 8 The Future of Leasing in the UK

The future of leasing and its role in the economy are difficult to assess with precision in the wake of the 1984 Finance Act. The changes in the rates of capital allowances and Corporation Tax announced in the 1984 Budget have undoubtedly had an unprecedented impact in stimulating the growth of leasing in the UK in the transitional period, but the removal of most of the tax advantage at the end of March 1986 is likely to precipitate a contraction in leasing activity in the short term. The position in the longer term is somewhat indeterminate and will largely be dependent upon the way in which the market adapts both in terms of supply and demand to the changes in the tax structure.

## 8.1 LESSORS

### 8.1.1 Market Structure

Both the surveys of lessors and lessees and wider discussion within the industry suggest a number of fundamental changes in the structure of the leasing market resulting from tax reform. Some of these changes are already apparent and others will become manifest as the market fully adjusts to the effects of the 1984 Finance Act. As we have previously indicated, the leasing industry is essentially heterogeneous and consequently the impact of changes in the tax structure on any particular segment will depend upon the degree to which tax advantage has been an important factor in determining past growth and development.

Lessors which have entered the market primarily as a tax sheltering device have been led to reappraise their leasing activity and have examined the alternatives of diversifying within the market or leaving it completely. Those that leave the market will tend to be firms in the non-financial sector whose motivation to become lessors has been widely determined by tax advantage alone. There is some evidence to suggest movement amongst non-financial lessors away from the market, but at the same time there have been indications that this

145

movement is by no means general and some diversification has occurred.[1] In addition to lessors outside the financial sector, non-British banks which have engaged in leasing purely as a taxation strategy are thought to have left the market. Conversely, foreign-owned lessors, which as a result of limited UK profits have not previously benefited to the same degree as domestic lessors from the system of capital allowances, are expected to expand their activities as they are able to compete on more equitable terms. Equally, foreign lessors which have not previously engaged in leasing in the UK may now consider the market suitable for expansion of their overseas activities.

## 8.1.2  Sectoral Differences

The effects of the 1984 Finance Act will be felt least in the small-ticket sector of the market because tax considerations have been generally less important in such transactions. This area of the market has been largely comprised of sales-aid leasing where the use of leasing has been essentially as a marketing tool. Although tax advantage has been of some significance to the lessor, the actual lease–buy decision from the perspective of the potential lessee tends to have been principally determined by non-tax-based factors. There are several reasons why this has been the case. Assets leased in this segment of the market are often small items, such as office equipment, and the tax implications on relatively small value assets are unlikely to be of consequence to the lessee. Similarly, as a result of expenditure size, cost of finance considerations may not be a major factor and no formal evaluation techniques employed. Lessees will tend to be primarily concerned with advantages of leasing such as convenience, fixed finance and flexibility. Other factors might include repair and maintenance agreements and the availability of upgrading facilities (i.e. the replacement of an existing leased asset with a new asset before the expiry of the lease term) which will safeguard against obsolescence. Sales-aid leasing ranges from a situation where the vendor of assets might simply recommend a particular leasing company to a customer, to manufacturers owning their own leasing subsidiaries. Between these extremes there is a varying degree of participation by the vendor which may, for example, involve him acting on behalf of the lessor in underwriting lease agreements. It is therefore often the case that leasing facilities are offered by equipment salesmen whose primary objective is to secure a sale rather than to develop an advanced level of expertise in financing alternatives. Indeed, evidence from the survey of lessors suggests that certain assets are sold only through leasing and no alternative methods of finance are offered. Consequently, because of the lack of dominance of tax-based leasing in the small-ticket sector, it is unlikely to be severely affected by the removal of tax advantage. On the contrary, it is expected that small ticket sales-aid leasing will expand. This is discussed in a following section on diversification.

The medium ticket sector, however, is likely to be more seriously affected by the provisions of the 1984 Finance Act. Although some medium ticket leasing is essentially sales-aid, this is not an important characteristic of this sector. Medium ticket leasing is principally a pure financing arrangement and is consequently sensitive to cost of finance considerations. By removing much of the tax advantage, in the absence of compensatory activities by lessors such as the acceptance of greater residual value risk, the implication of the 1984 Finance Act is that leasing rates will rise and move more into line with other borrowing rates. The relative competitiveness of leasing will thus diminish. In these conditions there is likely to be a movement away from leasing to other forms of finance, such as industrial hire purchase or bank loans, which are now able to provide many of the non-tax benefits of leasing. In addition to advantages of fixed terms and fixed rates, hire purchase facilities are available which require minimal deposits and structured repayments according to customers' requirements. In recent years, there have been significant developments in bank lending which have included moratorium periods for repayments until an asset is generating sufficient revenue and the gearing of repayments to seasonal cash flow fluctuations. Thus, it can be expected that a relative decline will occur in this sector as tax advantage diminishes and other forms of finance become increasingly attractive. The demand for traditional finance lease structures will fall away and it will be necessary for the industry to develop alternative structures such as the inclusion of operating lease elements to maintain a presence in the market. Clearly, the magnitude of decline is largely a function of the importance of tax advantage. However, there is likely to be a time lag before the full effects of the 1984 Finance Act are felt. Devereaux and Mayer (1984, p. 34), in their study of the impact of tax reform, have estimated that in 1982 50.2 per cent of companies in their sample were tax exhausted and have forecast, taking into account the changes in tax structure, that this will fall to 21.1 per cent by 1992. As Morris (1984, p. 46) has observed 'nearly a quarter of all companies will, on the basis of . . . [the] . . . estimates, still be in a position where leasing will provide a significant tax advantage'.

The position in the big ticket sector is somewhat unclear. Again, the future will be largely influenced by the past significance of tax considerations. Evidence from the survey of lessors indicates that tax considerations have in fact been important in this sector of the market both in terms of the supply of funds from lessors and the demand for leasing facilities by lessees. In view of this, it can be expected that the market will contract as a result of the tax gains from the leasing transaction becoming more marginal for lessor and lessee. However, even with only a 25 per cent writing down allowance there can be a tax advantage to leasing over longer terms which are common in big ticket transactions. In addition, timing advantages will remain. Lessors with subsidiary companies with year ends spread throughout the year may be able to obtain the benefit of allowances before the lessee, and on large transactions this can be advantageous. Nevertheless, even though some tax advantage will remain and not all transactions have been totally tax based, it is clear that the effect of the 1984 Finance Act will reduce the cost advantage of leasing in comparison to other forms of finance. In these circumstances large projects totally financed by leasing will become less common but leasing may still have a part to play as part of an overall project-financing 'package'. In addition, leasing may be made more attractive by the use of alternative structures such as non-recourse leveraged leasing discussed earlier in the lessor survey. With the complexity of arranging large-scale finance, it is likely that the skills and experience of lessors and the sophisticated financing arrangements they are able to offer will be required to some degree in the future.

### 8.1.3   Diversification

We have already mentioned that small ticket sales-aid leasing, is likely to expand as it has been a profitable activity for lessors and not wholly dependent on tax advantage. Already there has been considerable interest shown by lessors in this type of leasing,[2] but its expansion will clearly be determined by the overall level of demand for sales-aid facilities and the ability of lessors, diversifying into sales-aid leasing from other sectors, to adapt to the rather specialised nature of the market. Items of equipment leased are relatively small and typically include assets such as office equipment or vending machines. A relatively large volume of business is therefore required for successful operation and this tends to involve more administration than has been the case in other market sectors. This may necessitate the establishment of branch networks where they do not already exist and the employment of suitably skilled administrators. In addition to administrative factors, sales-aid leasing tends to entail higher risk-taking on the part of lessors than in many other areas of leasing activity, largely because of the size and characteristics of the assets leased and nature of lessees. In the past, much of sales-aid leasing has been structured on the basis of finance leasing. However, specialist skills are required to a degree perhaps not previously encountered, not only in assessing the creditworthiness of customers, which may be relatively small firms without a proven 'track record', but also in assessing the resale value of small items should the lessor default. Sales-aid leasing is unlikely to be pure finance leasing and is likely to involve the provision of services such as maintenance and repair of the asset. Furthermore, it is increasingly common for the lessor to offer upgrading facilities. This form of leasing is somewhat of a hybrid, containing elements of both finance and operating leasing, although there has recently been some movement in the market towards the increased use of operating-type agreements. Thus although sales-aid leasing provides an attractive area for diversification by lessors hitherto primarily engaged in tax based finance leasing in other sectors, direct entry into the market (rather than acquiring existing sales-aid leasing companies) is by no means straightforward, as very different operating structures and skills are necessary.

Operating leasing is a further potential area of expansion in a market where there is little tax advantage. The reasons for this are not difficult to determine. Operating leasing has tended to be far less sensitive to tax considerations than finance leasing. Operating lessors typically specialise in a range of specific assets and pass on the benefits of specialist knowledge and large-scale purchase of assets to lessees. At the same time the risks of ownership, in particular those associated with technological change, are borne by the lessor. As we saw in the Introduction, operating lessors' profits may arise in a number of ways – from re-leasing the asset; from selling the asset; and from the provision of ancilliary services. In these circumstances, unlike finance leasing, residual value is of the utmost importance. Advantages to the lessee from operating leasing therefore include risk reduction, the benefits of the lessors' specialist skill and economies of scale in purchasing, servicing arrangements and advantageous rental structures as a result of the lessor taking account of the residual value of the asset. With the diminishing significance of tax advantage and consequent increase in relative cost when compared with alternative forms of finance, leasing may be made a more attractive option by lessors generally assuming a higher risk of the residual value of assets and building this into the rental structure. The provision of a total service in addition to the finance function may also prove increasingly attractive.

Further impetus towards operating leasing has been provided by the publication of SSAP 21 which requires that finance leases but not operating leases should be disclosed in the balance sheet of the lessee. Firms which prefer to keep leasing commitments 'off balance sheet' may therefore be drawn towards operating leasing.

However, as with sales-aid leasing, there are difficulties in lessors entering the market without previous experience. Operating leasing is essentially the provision of a range of services to the customer which is not limited only to finance and in view of this, together with the importance of residual values, it is necessary to possess a considerable degree of specialist knowledge of assets and asset markets. Lack of knowledge of asset values may be partially offset by insuring against loss on residual value but in the past this type of insurance has tended to be relatively expensive. There also remains the question of expert technological knowledge of assets which may be resolved only by the acquisition of existing operating leasing companies or the employment of specialist personnel with experience in the market.

As well as diversifying leasing activities, lessors are likely to place a greater emphasis upon hire purchase as an alternative form of instalment credit. As we have seen previously, many of the advantages claimed for leasing are equally applicable to hire purchase, particularly in terms of cash flow, and it may be argued that its past growth has been limited by the fact that there was such a clear advantage to leasing. The survey of lessor suggests that leasing companies are giving careful consideration to the expansion of hire purchase but this is difficult to quantify. The Equipment Leasing Association does not currently analyse the non-leasing business of its members and official statistics do not separate out industrial hire purchase, so it is difficult to identify the extent of any switch away from leasing.

The effects of diversification by existing lessors may well be a polarisation in the market with some companies operating in specialised areas whilst others will offer leasing as part of a much wider range of financial services.

## 8.2   LESSEES

We have dealt with the likely effects of the 1984 Finance Act for lessors at some length because significant adjustments are necessary to accommodate the major reform of the tax structure. The position of the lessee is somewhat more difficult to assess as direct evidence of possible future trends is much less discernible.

### 8.2.1   Demand

Evidence from the survey of lessees suggests that there will be a marked decline in the demand for leasing facilities. Although many firms were still undecided on the future use of leasing at the time of the survey, 32.8 per cent of respondents in the South West survey and 50.0 per cent of respondents to the NIESR survey indicated that other forms of finance would be used instead of leasing. Bank borrowing and hire purchase were indicated as the main alternatives. It is interesting to note that in the South West survey a larger proportion of firms indicated more use of finance leasing (22.0 per cent) than operating leasing (16.1 per cent) in the future. It may well be that such firms have not fully appreciated the implications of tax reform. On the other hand, most of the leasing activity will tend to be small ticket leasing, particularly of vehicles and office equipment, which is largely non-tax based. Partial support for the latter view comes from the fact that tax advantages were ranked below avoiding large capital outlay in the analysis of factors taken into account when deciding to lease. In contrast, a major proportion of respondents from the NIESR survey panel of larger firms, which prima facie are likely to have a relatively high degree of sophistication in financial decision-making, indicated the use of more operating than finance leasing in the future (19.2 per cent) rather than the reverse (7.7 per cent). In addition, tax advantage was the most cited reason for leasing by respondents.

Although strict comparison between the two samples is clearly not possible, it would appear that the effects of the 1984 Finance Act will have less impact on small firm leasing which tends not to be so tax sensitive as the leasing activity of larger firms. The implications for the industry are serious. On the premise that the bulk of leasing transactions for smaller firms tends to be small ticket and medium and big ticket leasing tends to be principally undertaken by larger firms, even though small ticket leasing is generally high volume business in terms of value, it is likely to form only a relatively small proportion of total leasing. The evidence suggests that contraction as a result of diminished tax advantage will be most prevalent in the medium and big ticket sectors where the value of business transacted is likely to be greater.

### 8.2.2 Effects on the Distribution of Leasing Activity

Market adjustment by lessors to the 1984 Finance Act and contraction of the demand for tax-based leasing facilities are likely to give rise to changes in the sectoral distribution of leasing business. Previously the market has been dominated by the manufacturing sector. Given the movement towards small ticket sales-aid and operating leasing and the types of asset, such as office equipment, computers and vehicles which tend to be prevalent in these forms of leasing, then it can be expected that more emphasis will be put on leasing in the service sector. This will not be totally a product of changes in the tax structure for in recent years the service sector of the economy has expanded and attracted the attention of lessors before the 1984 Finance Act. The effect will therefore be to accelerate an existing trend.

Changes in sectoral distribution will also be reflected in shifts in the distribution of types of asset leased. Clearly movement away from the manufacturing sector will produce a decline in the leasing of plant and machinery. Evidence to support this is provided from the experience in other countries where leasing has not been heavily influenced by tax advantage. In West Germany, for example, service industries in 1982 accounted for some 47 per cent of assets acquired by members of the German Leasing Association, BDL, and office equipment, computers and vehicles represented 43 per cent of assets acquired analysed by type of asset.[3]

## 8.3 IMPLICATIONS

There is little doubt that as a result of the 1984 Finance Act the future of leasing in the UK is uncertain. The combination of the expansion of tax investment incentives and the increasing incidence of tax exhausted firms, together with rising inflation and interest rates, created the conditions for rapid growth in leasing from the mid 1970s onwards. Leasing has grown through periods of recession and our evidence supports the hypothesis that it has not only affected the quantity of investment in the economy but has also acted in a counter-cyclical manner. Now that tax reform and counter-inflationary measures have effectively removed the conditions for such growth, the short-run effect is likely to be a contraction in leasing in the UK. It is difficult to make a clear assessment of the precise magnitude of the contraction at this stage. Undoubtedly a large proportion of the rapid increase in leasing investment since the implementation of the 1984 Finance Act represents a bringing forward of expenditure to gain the remaining tax advantages, and a significant decrease in investment both through leasing and other methods of finance would therefore be expected in the period after April 1986 from this cause. Thus the rise in leasing activity in 1984–5 and 1985–6 is to a large extent 'abnormal' because of the changes in taxation and, in the same way, leasing activity in 1986–7 is likely to be abnormally low because of the earlier bringing forward of investment. Consequently, it is not before 1987–8 that a clear picture of the effects of tax changes will begin to emerge. However, the experience of the Swedish leasing industry, when tax credits were removed in 1984, suggests that, unless there is a marked expansion in non-tax-based leasing to offset the import of tax changes, the initial downturn could be very substantial. Clearly this will have significant implications for the level of investment and future growth in the UK economy. Nevertheless, the large size of the increases in business in the transition period must lead one to question whether the industry is being too pessimistic about the longer run prospects.

The longer term position is a little more difficult to assess. The short-run contraction in leasing activity may be reversed by the development of new products and expansion of non-tax-based leasing but, as we have seen, these are very different in nature from the tax-based finance leasing which has had important effects on the investment behaviour of firms and the economy as a whole. The economic impact of non-tax-based leasing is therefore not likely to be as significant. Evidence from other countries shows that although leasing has grown in conditions where tax advantage has not been an important factor, the contribution to investment has been smaller and counter-cyclical effects have not been particularly marked. Nevertheless, care should be taken not to overestimate the effects of the removal of much of the tax advantage of UK leasing. Albeit to a lesser degree, leasing has actually penetrated the financing of capital expenditure in countries where there are few tax advantages. Clark's estimates, shown in an earlier chapter, indicate, for example, that leasing accounted for some 8.5 per cent of capital formation in France in 1982. There is no reason to expect that the eventual position in the UK would be any lower than in such countries. Indeed, it may remain considerably higher as both lessees and lessors are used to the activity and will thus tend to continue, especially since the effect of the 1984 Finance Act is to make other sources of external finance no more attractive than leasing. It merely removes much of leasing's tax advantage. In addition, it is also important to consider the position of lessors in relation to leasing business already transacted. Lessors will have assets which have been depreciated rapidly for tax purposes. If these are subsequently sold this could have a major effect on their tax position if further assets are not acquired. There may therefore be an incentive for lessors to continue or indeed expand their leasing activity.

Thus although the leasing industry will remain as a source of finance for asset acquisition, and its history of innovation is likely to ensure that it will be able to adapt to changed market conditions, the exact nature and size of the future leasing market remains in question. In any event, because of the past domination of the market by subsidiaries of the major clearing banks, the overall effect of the 1984 Finance Act will depend largely on how they react. In addition to the survey of lessees, the evidence presented here tends substantially to reflect the initial views of such lessors. These views may alter significantly as practical adaptation to the changing market develops.

# 9 Conclusions

## 9.1 THE HYPOTHESES

The hypotheses put forward in this research suggested that the growth of leasing has had a favourable macroeconomic effect on the UK economy in two ways. First, by providing a relatively cheap source of finance through tax advantage it has led to a higher level of investment than would otherwise have been the case. This investment, particularly in view of its concentration on plant and equipment, is likely to have generated a faster rate of growth, both through increasing capacity and reducing costs, hence aiding competitiveness and increasing the UKs ability to export overseas and to substitute against imports.

Second, by allowing companies that were tax exhausted to finance investment on terms which were comparable to those for non-tax exhausted companies, leasing has altered the timing of investment in relation to fluctuations in the level of economic activity. Since tax exhaustion tends to occur in periods of low profitability traditionally associated with recessions, leasing has thus acted as a counter-cyclical force in the economy. This is advantageous to the economy not only because it reduces fluctuations in activity but also because it enables more investment to be undertaken in a downturn which can then stimulate and accelerate recovery. One of the main reasons for the cyclical nature of economic activity is that investment can have the effect of amplifying the cycle by bringing increased capacity into use at the end of the boom, hence generating excess output, which can only be reduced by massive destocking. Evidence on investment functions[1] suggests that time lags in investment are usually of the order of eighteen months to two and a half years, although those for large projects can be considerably longer, whilst investment in small items of capital is likely to be completed almost immediately. When cycles are four to five years in duration the bringing forward of investment expenditures could clearly have a marked effect on the stability of economic growth.

## 9.2   THE EVIDENCE

There is little doubt that the two principal hypotheses are substantiated by the evidence. What is more difficult to determine is the precise extent of the significance of tax implications within the overall growth of leasing and its effects upon the pattern and level of investment. The survey evidence from lessors has largely indicated that leasing has both increased the level of investment and brought forward its timing. However, lessors were generally unable to quantify these effects. In addition, the evidence drawn from this source suggests that, although tax advantage has been a major determinant in these processes, other benefits derived by firms from leasing have been significant. In contrast, the survey of lessees has shown that, despite the general acknowledgement of the importance of tax advantage in the decision to lease, the majority of respondents in both samples felt that leasing has had little effect either on the quantity or timing of investment. Of the firms that offered an explanation of why this should be the case, it was commonly indicated that financing and investment decisions were taken separately. Furthermore, many respondents commented that investment decisions were determined by factors such as the level of demand or operational requirements and that investment would have been financed merely by the utilisation of alternative sources in the absence of leasing (or at least the tax-based element of it). Thus the results of the survey of lessees are very much in line with much of the previous survey evidence on the effects of investment incentives presented in Chapter 5, which has generally indicated a weak influence on investment behaviour.

Consequently, the evidence drawn from the surveys tends to be somewhat inconclusive. As might be expected from using survey techniques, the data obtained at the microeconomic level on the relative strengths of the different ways in which leasing might affect investment and the magnitude of its effect do not present a particularly clear picture. Although both acknowledge the importance of tax advantage, on the one hand the evidence from lessors suggests leasing has had a significant impact on investment, whilst on the other the survey of lessees indicates only a very weak effect. However, two factors militate against the latter. The first is the econometric evidence which shows a very strong surge in investment over the period of rapid growth in leasing, varying from half the size of the leasing-based investment to more than twice it. It was very clear to one of the authors, who was leading the forecast team at the National Institute of Economic and Social Research at the time, that investment was running well ahead of its traditional determinants. While leasing was not the only change in behaviour taking place at the time, it was by far the most obvious one. The second factor is the way in which leasing has reacted to the 1984 Finance Act with a 39 per cent rise in 1984 over the previous year and a corresponding 43 per cent rise in 1985 (based on Equipment Leasing Association figures for assets acquired at cost by its members in current prices unadjusted for changes in membership). This shows that short-run impacts can be quite considerable and movements to take advantage of cost differentials large.

In a separate study by Levis *et al* (1985), the long-run impact of the tax changes on the level of fixed investment by industrial and commercial companies has been estimated to be a reduction of the order of 4 per cent, compared to what it would have been under the tax system and economic circumstances prevailing before the 1984 Budget. Although there is a clear distinction between industrial and commercial companies (i.e. largely non-financial private companies) and manufacturing companies, as an indication of the likely effect of leasing it is possible to infer from this that since leasing formed about 20 per cent of investment in new assets employed by manufacturing companies in the period before the 1984 Finance Act, this implies that around 20 per cent of leasing led to an increase in investment not a substitution between sources of finance. However, tax-based leasing was not the only motivation and hence the figure of 20 per cent is likely to be an underestimate.

## 9.3 THE MACROECONOMIC IMPACT

In our simulations of how important these results are for the economy, we have taken as an example the impact on the economy if only half of leasing led to increased investment rather than substitution. While this is larger than the smallest estimates of the impact, it is still well within the limits of the larger ones. From these we see that by 1985 leasing had led to investment some 17 per cent higher than it would otherwise have been, a rather stronger result than that suggested by Levis *et al* (1985). This higher level of investment in turn increased the rate of economic growth leading to GDP some 2 1/2 per cent higher at the end of the period and unemployment over 300 000 lower. However, the increased demand contributed to the rate of price inflation, which led to a price level some 20 per cent higher. As a consequence there were substantial feedback effects in the economy and real incomes and consumption might have been 1–1 1/2 per cent higher in the absence of leasing. This would have represented an even harsher pressure on real profitability.

Leasing thus gave a substantial boost to economic growth, but its rate of rise was so strong that the extent to which leasing enabled tax exhausted companies to invest, at the margin, is difficult to disentangle. Leasing continued to increase investment strongly through the recession of 1980–1 and as a result contributed to shortening its length and reducing its depth.

The full impact of leasing in its previous form will, however, not be calculable as the 1984 Finance Act resulted in a major disturbance to the determinants of leasing before leasing's long-run role in financing investment had become clearly established.

## 9.4   THE FUTURE

The restructuring of the corporate tax structure implemented in the 1984 Finance Act has had serious implications for the future of leasing and its contribution to the UK economy. As we have seen, the immediate impact of this legislation has been to give rise to a rapid surge in leasing activity. This is probably only a short-run effect, and the question remains as to what the future of leasing is likely to be when the market has fully adjusted to the removal of most of the tax-based advantage, and, furthermore, what the implications will be for the economy as a whole.

Throughout the present study, we have attempted to distinguish the effects of tax incentives on the growth of leasing and its impact on investment from other sources of influence. Clearly, while the tax motive may be the most important, it is not the only one. Lessors in the sales-aid and operating lease sectors, for example, have not been totally motivated by tax advantage. Equally, there is also considerable evidence, not only from the current study but also from previous research as indicated in Chapter 4, to suggest that the decision by lessees to lease assets is not determined by tax implications alone. Cash flow related advantages have certainly been regarded by lessees as a principal factor in the leasing decision. Other important reasons why firms lease assets have included, for example, the flexibility of leasing; off-balance sheet characteristics; and the provision of an additional source of finance. Evidence from our survey of lessees suggests that, taking into account both examples, at most, around half of the leasing decisions undertaken by respondent firms in the periods under consideration have been influenced by tax advantage. On this premise the fall in demand for leasing facilities and subsequent contraction of the market could be very substantial. Indeed, evidence from other countries suggests that a fall of this scale would reduce UK leasing to the average of other European countries where tax advantage has not been such an important factor. However, there are several reasons why a contraction of this magnitude is unlikely to occur. Leasing has developed over a relatively long period and is now widely accepted by firms as an important method of asset finance. Given the degree of market penetration and the fact that not all leasing is tax based, then a rather smaller decline might be expected. Furthermore, some of the effects of the removal of much of the tax advantage of leasing will be offset by the introduction of new products and the expansion of lessors into areas such as operating leasing where tax advantage has not been important. Presumably there will be a serious contraction in the market but at present it is difficult to determine precisely how large it will be. Although tax advantage has been a key factor in the growth of leasing and its macroeconomic impact, leasing has developed in what are essentially non-tax-based environments. This industry has a history of innovation and adaptation to changing market conditions and, albeit in a somewhat different form, leasing will remain as a significant source of finance for firms.

Turning now to the impact that the changes in the corporate tax structure and a reduction in leasing activity are likely to have on the UK economy, two principal effects can be identified.

These effects involve the transition costs of moving to the new system and the pattern of investment in the long term. Transitional costs will be of three types. First, there will be a lowering of investment levels generally which prima facie will lead to a lower rate of economic growth and to more obsolete equipment. Secondly, there will be a change in the pattern of investment as companies are affected differently by the change in the tax and allowance system. Highly profitable companies with a substantial taxable capacity will have their profits increased and hence tend to invest more. At the lower end, tax exhausted companies may become taxpaying and hence find that the allowances on more of their investment actually reduce the relative cost of capital at the margin without leasing. On the whole, the effect will be mixed. It is not abundantly clear that this change will result in a marked improvement in the quality of investment as the government anticipates. In so far as it does, this quality effect may offset the quantity effect noted above.

The third aspect of the transition cost is that the phased introduction of the new scheme has encouraged leasing and investment markedly in the short run and will discourage it even more markedly in 1986 and 1987. Thus, while it was widely expected that the economy would begin to slow in 1984 and 1985, growth continued, aided in part by higher investment. The pressures continue into 1986 and 1987 and forecasts at the time of writing are still for a slow down.[2] Given that the pattern of five year cycles has been rather disturbed in the 1980s, first because of the sheer size of the UK's downturn and, second, because of the difference in timing between the UK and world recessions, it is not easy to assess the impact.

The tax changes will also affect the economy in the way that investment takes place in the longer run. It is hypothesised by the government that the change in the corporate tax system will lead to 'better' investment, in the sense of investment with a higher prospective real rate of return. If this proves to be the case, ex-post, then obviously for any particular level of investment the rate of growth of output subsequently will tend to be higher. Within this scenario it is to be expected that leasing will continue to play a role. In so far as leasing continued to increase investment, then the macroeconomic return would be greater. However, with considerably reduced margins over the costs of other forms of finance the marginal effect on investment is likely to be very small.

The more important question is whether the tax changes are a net benefit to the economy. Evidence is unclear, mainly because ex-ante rates of real return on investment tend to be very different from the rates revealed after the event. There are grounds for arguing that the gains from the new system are unlikely to match up to the gains that appear to have occurred from the rise of leasing, many of which will be lost under the new tax regime.

Nevertheless, some gains will continue to be reaped at the macro-economic level through the continuance of leasing. These include the more efficient allocation of resources and the increased pace of adoption of technical change. A simple example of the former occurs with the leasing of vehicle fleets which can be positioned, maintained and replaced much more flexibly through leasing. In the computing field, the advantage that leasing confers in being able to upgrade and replace equipment quickly is considerable.

This study has shown that leasing has had a significant impact upon the UK economy, not only by increasing the actual quantity of investment to a level above that which it would have been in its absence, but also by acting as a counter-cyclical influence during periods of recession. These effects have been largely, although not entirely, brought about by a tax structure which enabled lessors with taxable capacity to transfer much of the benefits of capital allowances (through reduced rentals) to tax exhausted firms, which were unable to take immediate advantage of such investment incentives. The 1984 Finance Act has effectively removed much of the tax advantage of leasing. Although under the new tax regime firms may still claim tax allowances, for example on plant and machinery in the form of a 25 per cent writing down allowance, in comparison to the allowances available under the pre-1984 system (i.e. 100 per cent first-year allowances in the case of plant and machinery), the gains from leasing will be substantially less. Consequently, it can be expected that once the effects of the upsurge in leasing activity, brought about by the transitional arrangements in phasing out first-year allowances and reducing the level of corporate taxation, have subsided, there will be a significant decline in leasing from this cause. The precise size of the downturn is difficult to assess at this juncture, but with the accelerated pace of leasing in the transitional period the short-run contraction could be substantial. The long-run position will be determined essentially by firms' reactions to the increase in the cost of leasing finance, caused by the changes in the system of corporate taxation and the eventual level of demand for largely non-tax-based leasing as a source of investment finance. Clearly, the evidence presented in this study suggests that a significant decline in the level of leasing activity brought about by the reform of the tax structure would have serious ramifications for the economy as a whole. However, tax allowances are not the only incentive to lease. Leasing will remain an attractive means of finance for many firms. In the longer run leasing will rise in response to the demand for investment. Thus the actual path to be observed for leasing over the rest of the decade will be the result of the combination of these influences and the competitive and innovative behaviour of the lessors. The surge of leasing in the transition period of the 1984 Finance Act may be a testament to the continuing potential strength of the industry rather than just a rush to get in before the larger gains disappear.

# Notes

## Preface

1. This allocation according to use rather than ownership has now become generally accepted. In future U.K. official statistics will follow it and company accounts will show it under the terms of SSAP2I.

## 1  Introduction

1. *British Business*, 8 June 1984, p. 173.
2. See, for example, Clark (1978), Tomkins, Lowe, and Morgan (1979) and Hubbard (1980A).
3. Brief examinations have been made by Clark (1978) pp. 52–3 and Tomkins, Lowe and Morgan (1979) pp. 75–87.
4. A brief summary of law relating to leasing in the UK is given in the *World Leasing Yearbook* (1985) p. 252 and is dealt with in more detail in Clark (1978) ch. 5.
5. In France, for example, under the contract of *crédit-bail* the lessee has the option to purchase the asset at the end of the lease at an agreed price.
6. Statement of Standard Accounting Practice No. 21, 'Accounting for Leases and Hire Purchase Contracts'. The Institute of Chartered Accountants in England and Wales, August 1984, Part 2 – Definition of Terms, para. 15.
7. See, Savage (1978).
8. See, for example, Fawthrop and Terry (1975), Sykes (1976) and Hull and Hubbard (1980).
9. Clark (1978) pp. 180–2. See also Ang and Peterson (1984).
10. Published in: (i) *The Bank of England Quarterly Bulletin*; (ii) *The United Kingdom National Accounts* – the CSO *Blue Book*; (iii) *British Business* (Department Of Trade and Industry). These data have been supplemented by information provided by the Business Statistics Office.

## 2  The Growth of Leasing in the UK

1. Clark (1978) p. 5. The analysis of the early growth of leasing in this section is largely based on Clark (1978) pp. 15–22.
2. Eighty per cent of the shares were held by Mercantile Leasing Company with United States Leasing Corporation holding the balance.
3. See Clark (1978) p. 17 and Drury (1982) p. 163.
4. Clark (1978) p. 19 (originally from Davis, E.W., 'Leasing and Factoring: A Study in Financial Innovation', *Credit*, 11, 1970, p. 70.
5. See, for example, Hull and Hubbard (1980).
6. The effects were not at first reflected in an increase in leasing activity because the switch to the imputation system of Corporation Tax did not

occur until April 1973. The immediate effect was to deter investment
because of pending changes in the rate of Corporation Tax. This is shown
in Table 2.3 where the finance leasing business of Equipment Leasing
Association members actually fell in 1972.

7. *Corporation Tax*, Cmnd 8456, 1982, p. 9, para. 4.7.
8. Income and Corporation Tax Act 1970.
9. See Edwards and Mayer (1983).
10. Edwards and Mayer (1983) have estimated, for example, that on average
    some 80 per cent of the tax advantage accrued to the lessee if in a
    permanently non-taxpaying position.
11. See Fawthrop and Terry (1975) p. 305; Sykes (1976) tables 11 and 12,
    pp. 20–1 and table 13, p. 25; Tomkins, Lowe and Morgan (1979) table
    8.4, p. 94; and Hull and Hubbard (1980) p. 628.
12. Tomkins, Lowe and Morgan (1979) p. 88.

## 4  The Use of Leasing by Firms

1. See Lund (1971) pp. 85–91.
2. Tomkins, Lowe and Morgan (1979) p. 83.
3. Hull and Hubbard (1980) p. 628.
4. Eisner (1957) p. 517.

## 5  Leasing and the Incentive to Invest

1. Rockley (1973) p. 248.
2. Melliss and Richardson (1976) p. 25.
3. Lund (1971) p. 88.
4. Lund (1971) p. 88.
5. See Lund (1971) p. 255.
6. Goodson and Gay Wenban-Smith are one and the same person,
   Wenban-Smith being her married name.
7. Burman (1970) p. 196.
8. See Field and Hills (1976).
9. 'Investment Incentives', Cmnd 4516, HMSO, 1970, para. 2 as quoted in
   'Corporation Tax', Cmnd 8456, 1982. op. cit. p. 95 para. 14.21.
10. The total number of companies was 4525 but the number varied for each
    individual year.
11. Devereux and Mayer (1984) table 5, p. 18 – A tax loss is defined as
    negative taxable profit, after deducting capital allowances, stock relief,
    net interest payments and taxable losses carried forward but before
    allowing for ACT or double taxation relief.
12. See Young (1984) for a discussion of the economic nature of the leasing
    market.
13. See Bank of England (1980), (1982) and (1985).
14. Bank of England (1980) p. 309.

## 6 Econometric Evidence

1. See Mayes (1981).
2. For example, see Jorgenson and Stephenson (1967).
3. The original equation has been respecified by adding a third lag on investment to make the equation dynamically stable, which it was not before.
4. See, for an example using the National Institute model, Britton A. (1986), 'Can Fiscal Expansion Cut Unemployment?', *National Institute Economic Review*, no. 115, February, pp. 83–99.

## 7 The Experience in Other Countries

1. See, 'Leasing and Investment', a report compiled on behalf of the Organisation for Economic Co-operation and Development (forthcoming) which includes a detailed analysis of the nature and availability of leasing statistics in member countries.
2. 'Penetration of Leasing in Capital Formation 1978–1982', compiled by Clark, T.M. and published in *World Leasing Yearbook* (1985), p. 19.
3. Special Report on Scandinavia, *Leasing Digest*, no. 107, October 1985, p. 41.
4. See Eckstein, W., 'Zur Statistischen Darstellung Und Erfassung Des Leasing', in Leasing, Beilage 7 zum Betriebs-Berater, Heft 13, Verlagsgesellschaft Recht und Wirtschaft mbH, 1985.
5. Big ticket transactions have tended to be tax oriented.
6. Reported in *Leasing Digest*, no. 104, June 1985.
7. AAEL *News Bulletin*, vol. 5, no. 5, June 1984, p. 4.

## 8 The Future of Leasing in the UK

1. *Leasing Digest*, no. 103, June 1985, p. 25.
2. *Leasing Digest*, no 99, February 1985, p. 5.
3. Figures include real-estate leasing.

## 9 Conclusions

1. See Mayes (1981).
2. See, for example, *National Institute Economic Review*, no. 117, August 1986.

# References

AGARWALA, R. and GOODSON, G.C. (1969) 'An Analysis of the Effects of Investment Incentives on Investment Behaviour in the British Economy', *Economica*, 36, November, pp. 377–88.

ALAM, K. and STAFFORD, L.W.T. (1985) 'Tax Incentives and Investment Policy: A Survey Report on United Kingdom Manufacturing Industry', *Managerial and Decision Economics*, 6, pp. 27–32.

ANG, P. and PETERSON, P.P. (1984) 'The Leasing Puzzle', *Journal of Finance*, September, pp. 1055–65.

BANK OF ENGLAND (1980) 'Equipment Leasing', *Bank of England Quarterly Bulletin*, 20, 3, pp. 304–10.

BANK OF ENGLAND (1982) 'Recent Developments In Equipment Leasing', *Bank of England Quarterly Bulletin*, 25, 4, pp. 382–9.

BANK OF ENGLAND (1985) 'Developments In Leasing', *Bank of England Quarterly Bulletin*, 25, 4, pp. 582–5.

BEAN, C.B. (1979) 'An Econometric Model of Manufacturing Investment in the UK', Government Economic Service Working Paper, No. 29.

BOATWRIGHT, B.D. and EATON, J.R. (1972) 'The Estimation of Investment Functions for Manufacturing Industry in the UK', *Economica*, 39, November, pp. 403–18.

BURMAN, J.P. (1970) 'Capacity Utilisation and the Determination of Fixed Investment', pp. 185–202 in Hilton, K. and Heathfield, D. (eds), *The Econometric Study of the United Kingdom, Macmillan*.

CLARK, T.M. *(1978) Leasing*, McGraw-Hill.

CONFEDERATION OF BRITISH INDUSTRY (1965) 'CBI Investment Incentives Survey', unpublished (cited in Lund (1971)).

CORNER, D.C. and WILLIAMS, A. (1965) 'The Sensitivity of Business to Initial and Investment Allowances', *Economica*, 32, pp. 32–47.

CORPORATION TAX (1982) Cmnd 8456, HMSO.

DEVEREUX, M.P. and MAYER, C.P. (1984) *Corporation Tax: The Impact of the 1984 Budget*, The Institute For Fiscal Studies Report Series, No.11.

DIETZ A. (1977) 'Marketing and Commercial Policy', paper presented to the Leaseurope Conference, Oslo.

DRURY, A.C. (1982) *Finance Houses*, Waterlow.

EDWARDS, J.S.S. and MAYER, C.P. (1983) *Issues In Bank Taxation*, The Institute for Fiscal Studies, Report Series, No. 5.

EISNER, R. (1957) 'Interview and Other Survey Techniques and the Study of Investment', pp. 513–84, in National Bureau of Economic Research Studies in Income and Wealth, vol. 19, *Problems of Capital Formation*, Princeton University Press.

FAWTHROP, R.A. and TERRY, B. (1975) 'Debt Management and the Use of Leasing Finance in UK Corporate Financing Strategies', *Journal of Business Finance and Accounting*, Autumn, pp. 295–314.

FAWTHROP, R.A. and TERRY, B. (1976) 'The Evaluation of an Integrated

Investment and Lease Finance Decision', *Journal of Business Finance and Accounting*, Autumn, pp. 79–111.

FEDERATION OF BRITISH INDUSTRIES (1960) Principal Memoranda of Evidence to the Committee on the Working of the Monetary System, vol. 2, HMSO.

FELDSTEIN, M.S. and FLEMMING, J. (1971) 'Tax Policy, Corporate Saving and Investment Behaviour', *Review of Economic Studies*, 38, pp. 415–34.

FIELD, G.M. and HILLS, P.V. (1976) 'The Administration of Industrial Subsidies', pp. 1–22, in *The Economics of Industrial Subsidies* (ed. Whiting, A.), Department of Industry, HMSO.

GEORGE, K. in collaboration with HILLS, P.V. (1968) *Productivity and Capital Expenditure in Retailing*, Cambridge University Press.

HART, H. and PRUSSMAN, D. (1964) 'A Report of a Survey of Management Accounting Techniques in the SE Hants. Coastal Region', unpublished (cited in Corner and Williams, 1965).

HOUSE OF LORDS (1985), *Overseas Trade*, Report from the Select Committee on Overseas Trade, HMSO.

HUBBARD, G.L. (1980 A) *Finance Leasing – A Guide for Lessees in the UK*, The Institute of Cost and Management Accountants.

HUBBARD, G.L., (1980 B) 'Leasing: The Cash Flow Myth', *Management Accounting*, February, pp. 24–6.

HULL, J.C. and HUBBARD, G.L. (1980) 'Lease Evaluation in the UK: Current Theory and Practice', *Journal of Business Finance and Accounting*, Winter, pp. 619–37.

JORGENSON, D.W. and STEPHENSON, J.A. (1967) 'Investment Behaviour in US Manufacturing 1947–60', *Econometrica*, 35, pp. 169–220.

KING, M.A. (1972) 'Taxation and Investment Incentives in a Vintage Investment Model', *Journal of Public Economics*, 1, pp. 121–47.

LEVIS, M., MORGAN. E.J. with O'LOAN, D. and THANASSOULAS, C. (1985) 'The 1984 Budget: Effects on Corporate Tax and Investment', University of Bath School of Management, Discussion Paper No. 67.

LUND, P.J. (1971) *Investment: The Study of an Economic Aggregate*, Oliver & Boyd.

MAYES, D.G. (1981) *Applications of Econometrics*, Prentice-Hall.

MAYES, D.G. and WENBAN-SMITH, G. (1981) 'The Macroeconomic Effects of Instalment Credit and Leasing', *Credit*, September, pp. 58–63

MORRIS, D.J. (1984) (ed.) *The Economic System in the UK*, Oxford University Press.

MELLIS, C.L. and RICHARDSON, P.W. (1976) 'Value of Investment Incentives for Manufacturing Industry 1946 to 1974', pp. 23–43, in *The Economics of Industrial Subsidies* (ed. Whiting, A.), Department of Industry, HMSO.

MINISTRY OF TECHNOLOGY (1970) *Investment Incentives Survey*, summarised in Hansard, 14 December, Written Answers, cls. 238–41.

NATIONAL ECONOMIC DEVELOPMENT COUNCIL (1965), *Investment in Machine Tools*, HMSO.

*National Institute Economic Review*, no. 117, August 1986.

ROCKLEY, L.E. (1973) *Investment for Profitability: An Analysis of the Policies and Practice of UK and International Companies*, Business Books.

SARANTIS, N.C. (1979) 'Relative Prices, Investment Incentives, Cash Flow, and Vintage Investment Functions for UK Manufacturing Industries', *European Economic Review*, 12, pp. 203–26.

SAVAGE, D. (1978) 'The Channels of Monetary Influence: A Survey of the Empirical Evidence', *National Institute Economic Review*, no. 83, February, pp. 73–89.

SYKES, A. (1976) 'The Lease–Buy Decision: A Survey of Current Practice in 202 Companies', Management Survey Report No. 29, British Institute of Management.

TOMKINS, C.R., LOWE, J.F. and MORGAN, E.J. (1979) *An Economic Analysis of the Financial Leasing Industry*, Saxon House.

WHITE, W.H. (1956) 'Interest Elasticity of Demand – The Case from Business Attitude Surveys Re-examined', *American Economic Review*, 46, pp. 565–87.

*World Leasing Yearbook* (1985), Hawkins.

YOUNG, C.M. (1984) 'The Competitiveness of Lease Markets: An Empirical Investigation of the UK Local Authority Lease Market', *Journal of Business Finance and Accounting*, Summer, pp. 189–98.

# Index

accelerated cost recovery
system 140–1
accelerator 107–8
agriculture 37, 41
Association Française des Sociétés
Financiers 133

*Bodembeslag* 138

capacity utilisation 110
capital allowances 1, 6, 9, 10, 15,
16, 22, 23, 24, 30, 34, 47, 75, 82,
146
capital expenditure 7
cars 20–1, 54–5
cash flow 1, 6, 7, 10, 34, 43, 52,
70, 74, 78, 94, 107, 110, 115, 142
Competition and Credit
Control 15
concentration ratios 101
corporation tax 1–2, 17, 23, 24, 96
advanced 17
cost of capital 108
*crédit-bail* 131–5
*immobilier* 132
*mobilier* 132
credit controls 15
creditworthiness 31, 36, 44, 50

debt capacity 8, 9, 19
debt–equity ratio 8, 9
decision-making 38–42

Economic Recovery Tax
Act 140–1
Equipment Leasing
Association viii, 11, 14, 16, 20,
21, 23, 28, 48, 52, 150, 157

Finance Act 1980 22
Finance Act 1984 ix, 1, 2, 11,
23–5, 33, 43, 62, 82–4, 112, 122,
125, 145–8, 151–4, 157, 158
finance houses 14, 15, 18, 103
France 129–35

gearing 33, 49
Green Paper on Corporation Tax
1982 17

hire purchase 4, 13, 35, 47, 132,
147

inflation 36, 37, 44
interest rates 10, 36, 37
investment ix, 3, 7, 9, 28, 38–9,
42–3, 57, 79
investment, distribution and
services vii, 119–22
investment grants 15, 16, 89, 97,
99–100
investment incentives 9, 11, 15,
82, 87–104
investment, manufacturing vii,
98–9, 110–8
Investment Tax Credits 129, 140
investment, timing of 79

Japan 50

lease brokers 40, 47, 103
lease finance 4–5, 18–19, 23, 46, 127
lease operating 5, 6, 18–19, 46,
127, 149, 150
leasing
definitions 3–5
captive 67
small, medium, large 'ticket' 20
leveraged leasing 46
non-recourse 148
Leverhulme Trust viii
liquidity effect 91, 93, 96, 99

marketing 38
multinationals 51

National Institute model vii, 109,
110, 119, 122, 125
National Institute of Economic and
Social Research 59, 61–8, 109,
156–7

*Index*

NEDO   40
net present value   40
Netherlands   138–9
non-recourse leveraged
  leasing   148
North Central Wagon
  Company   13

off-balance-sheet financing   7, 9,
  14, 52, 78, 136
overseas banks   40, 47

profitability effect   91, 93, 96, 99
profits   1, 2, 10, 17, 33, 37

Regional Development
  Grants   42–3, 51, 54
residual value   4, 5, 30, 31, 46, 53,
  56, 150
risk   6, 37

sales aid   20, 32, 39, 44, 47, 55,
  59, 80–82, 139, 146, 148–9

small firms   72, 74
SSAP 21   7, 8–9, 37, 52, 53, 55,
  150
stock appreciation   16

tax allowances   15–19, 87
Tax Equity and Fiscal
  Responsibility Act   141
tax exhaustion   2, 16, 101, 147
tax incentives   1–2, 11
taxable capacity   102
technological change   35, 50–1
trade cycle   9–10

USA   46–7, 139–43

variation clauses   44–5

West Germany   50, 135–8
writing down allowances   ix, 2, 23,
  44, 89

year-end   43